lonely planet

POCKET HAVANA

Katya Bleszynska

Contents

Plan Your Trip 4

Explore Havana 37

FROM LEFT: IULIAN URSACHI/SHUTTERSTOCK, ANNE CZICHOS/SHUTTERSTOCK

Havana Toolkit 148

Top: Museo Nacional de Bellas Artes (p54)
Bottom: El Malecón (p80)

★ Top Experiences

The Journey Begins Here

Ragged and romantic, heart-racing and sometimes headache-inducing, Havana is a paradox that leaves an impression. It's a hot, colorful capital still reeling from the Cold War era. It breathes momentous history and tear-jerking nostalgia, yet it's packed with cutting-edge culture and effortlessly cool people. Times have been extra tough of late, but the city's inhabitants – charismatic, crafty, and creative – fight to keep things pushing forward against a complex current. Imagine the waft of gasoline from ancient American cars, sea salt whipped up from the Malecón and ripe guava being touted from street carts. That's Havana.

Katya Bleszynska
@explorerpensadora
Based in Cuba, Katya is a writer who is passionate about telling the stories of underexplored and underestimated places. She has written on Cuba, El Salvador and Mexico for Lonely Planet.

Centro Habana (p71)
LJUPCO SMOKOVSKI/SHUTTERSTOCK

THE BEST

Historical Experiences

The story of Cuba is unique and remarkable, no matter your political persuasion. Havana is a historical wonderland at every turn, a living museum of old American cars, juxtaposing architecture and mighty fortresses.

Decipher Havana's history at **Museo de la Ciudad** (pictured), housed in the baroque Palacio de los Capitanes Generales. (p47)

Climb the ramparts of the **Parque Histórico Militar Morro-Cabaña**, a military park meets museum complex with two impressive forts from the colonial period. (p132)

Peek at an opulent former mansion and study its collection of objects associated with the life of Napoleon at the **Museo Napoleónico**. (p106)

Go for a drink at **Hotel Nacional**, an emblematic turreted hotel which has become synonymous with Havana's mafioso history of the 1950s. (p94)

Explore a literary legacy at **Museo Hemingway** (pictured), the former home and grounds of the American writer who lived in Havana for over two decades. (p140)

Right: Hotel Nacional (p94)

FROM LEFT: GUILLAUME ANGLERAUD/SHUTTERSTOCK, RUI LECA/SHUTTERSTOCK, ROSEN IVANOV ILIEV/SHUTTERSTOCK

THE BEST

Architecture Experiences

Havana is an architect's dream. The eclectic assemblage of buildings is an unabashed hybrid of styles, ideas and influences; you might see baroque, neoclassicism, Catalan modernism, American eclecticism and Soviet brutalism all on the same street.

Take in **Edificio Bacardí**, the art deco former headquarters of the rum giant that fell out of favor with the Revolution. (p61)

Meander down **El Paseo del Prado** (Paseo de Martí); you'll find incredible architecture everywhere. (p77)

Be dazzled by gold and marble at the **Capitolio Nacional**, a spectacular neoclassical legislative building with tours of its lavish interiors. (p74)

Marvel at the **Russian Embassy**, a dominating dagger-shaped embassy building encapsulating Havana's brutalist soviet influence. (p121)

Admire the **Instituto Superior de Arte**, an art academy built in 1961 but left half-finished. Wander around curious brick domes and walkways. (p122)

Edificio Bacardí (p61)

ALEXANDRE F FAGUNDES/SHUTTERSTOCK

THE BEST

Church Experiences

While seven decades of *socialismo* has no doubt had an impact on organized religion in Cuba, the city retains many outstanding churches. On the outskirts of Havana lie two which have syncretized with Cuba's Afro-Cuban religions.

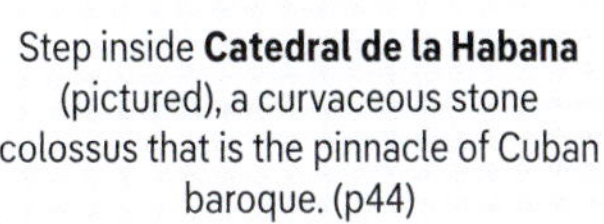

Step inside **Catedral de la Habana** (pictured), a curvaceous stone colossus that is the pinnacle of Cuban baroque. (p44)

Visit Cuba's second-largest church, the domed **Iglesia de Jesús de Miramar**, with its striking murals depicting the Stations of the Cross. (p121)

Make a pilgrimage to the far-flung **Santuario de San Lázaro**, dedicated to the patron saint of the poor and sick, known as Babalú Ayé in Afro-Cuban religions. (p137)

Gaze at the riot of frescoes and gilded trimmings of **Iglesia y Convento de Nuestra Señora de la Merced** (pictured), one of Havana's finest church interiors. (p60)

Cross Havana Bay to **Iglesia de Nuestra Señora de Regla**, a waterfront church dedicated to the Virgin of Regla, known as Yemayá, the deity of the ocean in the Afro-Cuban Santería religion. (p138)

FROM LEFT: KAMIRA/SHUTTERSTOCK, DIANA RITA CABRERA/LONELY PLANET

THE BEST

Art Experiences

Havana is most associated with dance and music, but it's underrated when it comes to art. The city's contemporary and independent art scene is very active, with endless artist studios and exhibitions to discover.

Walk around **Museo Nacional de Bellas Artes** (pictured) to take in the whole history of Cuban art supported by a commendable collection of international masterpieces. (p54)

Uncover contemporary art gallery **Galleria Continua** hidden in the heart of Centro Havana's Chinatown. (p86)

Lose yourself in the immense **Fábrica de Arte Cubano**, with probing, cutting-edge, always surprising art unleashed in this unique art 'factory.' (p98)

Visit **Fusterlandia** (pictured), a whole neighborhood covered in a giddy array of mosaics, tiles, and bright paintings. (p119)

Attend Havana's yearly **Bienal de la Habana** (p28) organized by the Wifredo Lam Institute, where you'll be surrounded by great art and the city's *farandula* (hip and arty crowd).

Right: Fábrica de Arte Cubano (p98)

FROM LEFT: TRUBA7113/SHUTTERSTOCK, CINEMATOGRAPHER/SHUTTERSTOCK, ALL CANADA PHOTOS/ALAMY

EL COCINERO
TIME
FAC

THE BEST

Nightlife Experiences

Although it no longer has a reputation as a casino capital city of sin, Havana's nightlife is still electric. Take your pick from high-quality cabaret, edgy rooftop parties, jazz concerts, salsa dancing and raucous reggaeton club nights.

A diamond in Habana Vieja's rough San Isidro neighborhood, **Yarini** puts on some of the best live music nights in the city and packed-out DJ sets. (p67)

Party like a young local Cuban at **King Bar**; it's always busy, open until very late and is reggaeton galore. (p105)

Basílica Menor de San Francisco de Asís is now a concert hall, which typically holds classical music recitals every Saturday late afternoon. (p46)

Enjoy a night out at **Fábrica de Arte Cubano** (pictured above left), a legendary cultural venue designed for diverse tastes, with catwalk shows, dance, fine art, cinema and live concerts of every genre imaginable. (p98)

Enjoy world-class Cuban jazz most nights of the week at **Fangio Habana** (pictured above) a rooftop restaurant and bar on Vedado's elegant Avenida Paseo. (p111)

Right: Yarini (p67)

FROM LEFT: HEMIS/ALAMY, FANGIO HABANA, YARINI HABANA

THE BEST

Bar Experiences

Step away from touristy Hemingway haunts and engage with Havana's modern bar scene. With more freedom to engage in private business, local entrepreneurs are directing their creativity into a growing number of dynamic drinking holes.

Order a piña colada or a gin and tonic at **El del Frente**, a fun rooftop bar and restaurant where drinks are served with flamboyant garnishes. (p67)

People watch with a mojito in hand at the relaxed **El Dandy** (pictured), which overlooks the bustling Plaza del Cristo. (p66)

Lounge at **El Bleco**, Havana's most expensive and exclusive bar with the best cocktails in the city and a live DJ music set against an ocean backdrop. (p89)

Enjoy a nightcap and a few rounds of dominoes at **El Bejuco**, a leafy and low-lit after-hours bar. (p113)

Swim, sunbathe and sip cocktails at **MAREA**, a beach bar overlooking Marina Hemingway where you can dive straight into the sea from your table. (p124)

Right: El del Frente (p67)

FROM LEFT: HYBBGO/SHUTTERSTOCK, LENA-WURM/SHUTTERSTOCK, HEMIS/ALAMY

M1
Coca-Cola

THE BEST

Dining Experiences

Havana's eating scene has progressed exponentially since the early 2010s despite perennial challenges such as procuring ingredients. Culinary experimentation has also proliferated. The most condensed activity is in Habana Vieja while Playa has the most exclusive restaurants.

For hearty Cuban food with a home-cooked feel, pass by **Doña Eutimia**, a cute and comforting establishment next to Plaza de la Catedral. (p64)

Indulge at Havana's most iconic restaurant, **La Guarida** (pictured), one of the city's first private restaurants and location for the film *Fresa y Chocolate*. (p78)

A nod to Cuba's European roots, **Toros y Tapas** does stellar Spanish cuisine, mixed with live flamenco and fine wine. (p124)

Climb an old factory tower and step out into **El Cocinero**, a swanky rooftop restaurant next door to Havana's hottest club, Fábrica de Arte Cubano. (p112)

Tuck into the freshest of fish along the river at **Santy Pescador**, a hidden, out-of-town location and former favorite of Fidel Castro. (p124)

Right: El Cocinero (p112)

THE BEST

Foodie Experiences

While there are some great restaurants in Havana, the best way to experience the food scene at its most authentic is to spend some time in the markets, small businesses and home kitchens of locals.

Discover the Afro-Cuban influence on the country's cuisine in a hands-on cooking class with **Beyond Roots** (pictured), preparing dishes in a local's kitchen in Guanabacoa. (p145)

Learn to make classic Cuban dishes at **La Lore Cooking Experience** (p58) with the star of TV cooking show *Lorena* in her rooftop alfresco kitchen.

Let **Jibaro** take you on a food tour around the markets of Habana Vieja, finishing up with mojito making and lunch at their restaurant. (p59)

Food shop like a local at **Mercado Agropecuario 19 y B**, a bustling Vedado fruit and veg market that gives an inside look into how Cubans buy their ingredients. (p109)

Head to **Bacoretto** (pictured), a family farm which follows an entirely vegan and gluten-free philosophy and puts on mouth-watering lunchtime feasts of creative and colorful vegan food. (p145)

Right: Mercado Agropecuario 19 y B (p109)

FROM LEFT: ANDY BRAVO, VIA BEYOND ROOTS, BACORETTO, SALVADOR AZNAR/SHUTTERSTOCK

Col
Melon
P Fruta

THE BEST

Shopping Experiences

Not too long ago, shopping in Havana consisted of buying a bottle of rum and a printed Che Guevara T-shirt. But now there are numerous places to buy interesting clothing, souvenirs, and other relics from independent sellers and stores.

Buy a statement tee, tote bag or cap from the trailblazing **Clandestina** (pictured), renowned for its catchy motifs, youthful designs and recycled materials. (p67)

Step inside **Centro de Las Raíces**, a store and salon specializing in all things Afro-Cuban, including clothing, hair products and accessories. (p67)

Treat yourself to a multicolored creation from **AMA Havana**. These two female designers make out-there (and barely there) beaded and crochet garments. (p113)

Browse the racks of **Calore**, a concept store marrying several of Havana's fashion brands under one highly glamorous roof. (p67)

Purchase a Cuban cigar from the **Real Fábrica de Tabacos Partagás Store** (pictured), affiliated to Havana's famous tobacco factory. (p68)

Peruse around **Feria de Publicaciones y Curiosidades**, an antiques market and treasure trove of fascinating relics. (p68)

FROM LEFT: CAROLYNE PARENT/SHUTTERSTOCK, ROBERTO LA ROSA/SHUTTERSTOCK

Best for Kids

Explore the two fabulous forts of **Parque Histórico Militar Morro-Cabaña** (p132) with long ramparts, dozens of old weapons, pirate history and a highly exciting after-dark cannon-firing ceremony.

Go for a coffee or lunch in the pretty **Plaza Vieja** (p42). A nearby primary school means that local children use the square as an unofficial playground at break times.

Visit the weird and wonderful world of **Fusterlandia** (p119), a fishing village turned into a Cuban tribute to Gaudí. It feels like what a child's drawing would like if they were asked to design their dream adventure playground.

Take a day trip to **Playas del Este** (p142) to find accessible sandy beaches just 20km east of Havana, with plenty of water toys available to rent.

Best for Free

Take a free walking tour of Old Havana's four main squares with *havanafreewalkingtour.com* or go at it alone. Many sites around the squares are free to visit, including Plaza de la Catedral's **cathedral** (p44).

Stroll along **El Malecón** (p80), an iconic sea promenade which is every Cuban's favorite free outing. Watch locals playing music, drinking rum, having romantic encounters and watching the sun set.

Get lost in the streets of **Centro Habana** (p71) – especially the main throughfares of Calle Galiano, Paseo del Prado and Bulevar de San Rafael – to do some good old-fashioned people watching.

Pop into the many free museums and stores along the pedestrianized **Calle Mercaderes** (p50), including a perfume shop, oriental-inspired Casa de Asia and an old gun shop turned museum.

Perfect Days

Take the morning slow with a Cuban coffee in the sun and a stroll before an action-pack afternoon of visiting old mansions, museums and monuments. Come nighttime, party like it's 1950s Havana in one of the city's many venues.

Classic car, Parque Central (p53)

FROM LEFT: ANGELBADA.PHOTOGRAPHY/SHUTTERSTOCK, ALARAX/SHUTTERSTOCK, AITOR RODRIGUEZ CLARO/ SHUTTERSTOCK, MELISSA HERZOG/SHUTTERSTOCK

DAY ONE

Only Have One Day?

MORNING

Start by heading to **Parque Central** (p53) and hopping in one of the numerous classic cars of your choosing for a ride around Havana, the best way to see the city's main sites if you're tight on time.

AFTERNOON

Explore Habana Vieja's four main colonial squares by foot, stopping for lunch in **Plaza Vieja** (pictured; p42) before heading down shop- and museum-lined **Calle Mercaderes** (p50). Cut through tree-filled **Plaza de Armas** (p47) on your way to the whimsical **Catedral de la Habana** (p44).

EVENING

For Habana Vieja's trendiest after-dark quarter, head to the **Plaza del Cristo** (p58), where a lively atmosphere pulsates in cool bars.

DAY TWO

A Weekend Trip

MORNING

Start with coffee in the **Plazuela de Santo Ángel** (p58). It's a short walk to **Capitolio Nacional** (p74), where you can take a morning guided tour of its opulent interiors.

AFTERNOON

Embrace Havana's art culture by visiting the Cuban collection of the **Museo Nacional de Bellas Artes** (p54). Afterwards, walk down **El Prado** (Paseo de Martí; p77) and turn left onto **El Malecón** (p80) sea drive to take in the sunset.

EVENING

After dinner, head over to the **Fortaleza de San Carlos de la Cabaña** (p132) for the famous Cañonazo ceremony (pictured; p135) at 9pm. Return to Habana Vieja for drinks and live music at bar **Yarini** (p67).

DAY THREE

A Short Break

MORNING

Start the day with a visit to Havana's magnificent cemetery, the **Necrópolis Cristóbal Colón** (pictured; p100). Walk over to the **Plaza de la Revolución** (p102) and the **José Martí Memorial** (p102).

AFTERNOON

Take a taxi to the **Universidad de la Habana** (p96) and also visit the nearby **Museo Napoleónico** (p106), an opulent ode to the French leader in a spectacular old mansion. Wander past Calle 23 before arriving just in time for a sunset mojito at **Hotel Nacional** (p94).

EVENING

Warm up with dinner and drinks at **El Cocinero** (p112) and spend the rest of evening at the incomparable **Fábrica de Arte Cubano** (p98).

If You Have More Time

Most people stick to Habana Vieja and Vedado when they have limited time, but if you want to get to the core of Havana, venture a little bit further. Sail Havana Bay on the local ferry to the Afro-Cuban neighborhoods of Regla and Guanabacoa, taking a tour with local experts **Regla Soul** (p144) or **Beyond Roots** (p145). Even further out, go on a personal pilgrimage to **Santuario de San Lázaro** (p137) to discover more about Santería and syncretism in Cuba.

Back in the city center, spend an afternoon going on a shopping trip in Habana Vieja, checking out the city's most trendy fashion brands in **Calore** (p67) and going hunting for antiques in **La Feria de Publicaciones y Curiosidades** (p68). The best thing to do in Havana is simply get lost walking through the different districts and noticing the little details in the architecture and street life that you may miss when you're in a rush.

Santuario de San Lázaro (p137)

POSSOHH/SHUTTERSTOCK

A City Day Trip

Go for breakfast at **El Café** (p64) before taking a taxi or tourist bus towards Habana del Este. Spend the day sunbathing, swimming and eating seafood at one of the areas idyllic beaches such as **Santa María del Mar** (p143) or **Mi Cayito** (p143).

On the way back, stop off at the entrance to **Parque Histórico Militar Morro-Cabaña** (p132), and stroll down to Casablanca's **Estatua de Cristo** (pictured above; p135) to take in mesmerizing views of Havana from the other side of the bay. Dine at **La Divina Pastora** (p147) and catch the 9pm canon-firing show at **Fortaleza de San Carlos de la Cabaña** (p135).

On a Rainy Day

Havana is best experienced in the open air and luckily rain showers tend to be fleeting (if furious), but there are some options for indoor experiences. Spend the day museum hopping at **Museo Nacional de Bellas Artes** (p54), **Museo de la Revolución** (p61) and **Capitolio Nacional** (pictured above; p74), all close by each other.

Indulge in some indoor dining at **La Guarida** (p78) and **San Cristóbal** (p88) in Centro Habana, **ChaChaChá** (p66) and **5 Sentidos** (p65) in Habana Vieja, and **La Corte del Príncipe** (p124) and **Sensaciones** (p125) in Playa. Order a taxi on La Nave app but if there is a major downpour you may need to wait until it clears up.

Get Prepared

BOOK AHEAD

Three months before Check visa requirements (especially if you're American), plan a general itinerary, book flights.

One month before Book hotels through travel agencies and/or contact casa particular owners regarding availability. Check with your bank to see if your ATM cards will work.

72 hours before Fill out your obligatory D'Viajeros (travel form) online information form *(dviajeros.mitrans.gob.cu)*.

Manners Matter

Life in Havana is very informal, so you won't hear as many pleases, thank-yous and sorrys as you do in other parts of the world. However, there is one essential form of social etiquette pertaining to queues. When joining a line, always ask '¿El último?' (who is the last person?) and make sure to keep an eye out for who is in front of you.

Cultural Norms

On one hand, men in Havana can be very chivalrous. They will give women a hand holding heavy items or help them get on and off transport. However, Cuban society is machista, and unwanted attention is very normalized. *Piropos* (catcalling), from the complimentary to the downright sexual, is part and parcel of life for women here. The best tactic is to always ignore.

Things to Know

Hustling Many locals have got *jineterismo* (hustling) down to a fine art, so watch out for the tricks. Common scams include currency exchange on the street, selling fake cigars and encouraging you to fall madly in love with them. Be very wary.

Alcohol measurements Many bars are very liberal with their alcohol pours, and with the amount of sugar in their cocktails it's easy to underestimate their rum content. Be especially careful in Fábrica de Arte Cubano (p98), where drinks are deceivingly strong.

Opening times Most attractions are closed on Monday, but timetables in general often change at a whim. Havana seems to come to a standstill when it rains, when events get cancelled and sites shut up shop. Even drivers call it a day.

TIPPING

Wages in Cuba are low, and a tip can make a huge difference.

Restaurants & cocktail bars
for good service

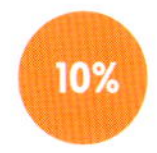

Drivers
for good service

Casa particular owners

Museums

DAILY BUDGET

Budget: Less than US$100

- Room at a casa particular: US$30–50
- Meal at a government-run restaurant: US$8–12
- Cheap museum entry: US$1

Midrange: US$100–200

- Room in a midrange hotel: US$50–120
- Meal in a private restaurant: US$12–20
- Mojito: US$3–4

Top end: More than US$200

- Room in a historic or boutique hotel: US$200–325
- City taxi: US$5–10
- Tropicana cabaret: US$95

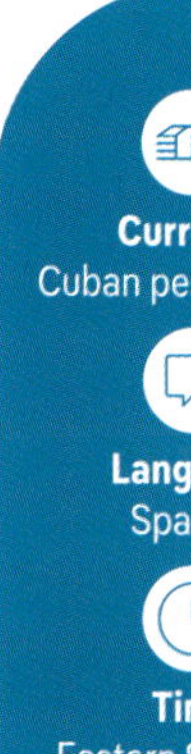

Currency
Cuban peso (CUP$)

Language
Spanish

Time
Eastern Standard Time (GMT/UTC minus five hours)

AHMED ZAGGOUDI/SHUTTERSTOCK ©

TIP

With wi-fi not always being easy to come by in Havana, purchasing a Cuban SIM card is a great way to stay connected when you're out and about. Buy online and pick it up at the airport, or go to an ETECSA office on arrival. Try the one on Calle M in the Focsa building (p108).

When To Go

The best season is between November and March. The heat is less oppressive, there's less chance of rain storms, and it's when Havana is at its busiest.

The end of the year is always Havana's liveliest time, with New Year's Eve being a big event while January 1 marks the anniversary of the triumph of the Cuban Revolution. From May through to October is low season, corresponding to rainy season. Expect brief but mighty showers every afternoon, and some serious humidity and heat. Havana starts to cool down from October, with a slight chill from the sea breeze at night time, but is still warm during the day.

The Big Events

January: The beginning of the year marks the hottest music festival in the city. Anyone who is anyone in the music world in Havana will be performing at the **Festival Internacional Jazz Plaza**, dedicated to jazz (and so much more).

February: If you like to dance, or love to watch it at least, **Festival De La Salsa** gathers *baile*-loving locals in popular indoor and outdoor venues to see Cuba's top salsa stars.

May 1: International Workers' Day (Día de los Trabajadores) is a big deal in Havana, where thousands of state workers and students get up at the crack of dawn to parade through Vedado to Revolution Square.

November–February: During peak season, every gallery and cultural space is filled with avant-garde artwork from both Cuban and international artists for the biennial **Habana Bienal**.

Havana Weather

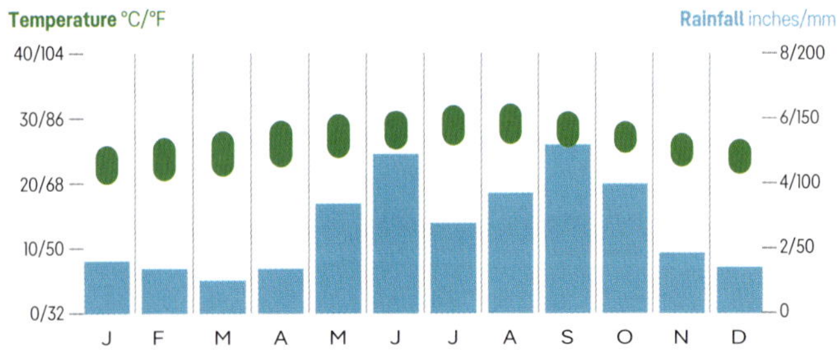

BERNA NAMOGLU/SHUTTERSOCK

International Workers' Day

Niche Fests

February: Havana's most prestigious event is without a doubt the **Festival del Habano**. Lovers of Cuban cigars flock from all over the world to high-end galas and exclusive dinners all geared around the country's most luxurious export. The ticket price is hefty.

February: **Feria Internacional del Libro de La Habana** is a literary festival set in the incredible location of Havana's La Cabaña fort (p132). This is the place to watch locals buy books, attend talks and spend time with their families.

October: Held every two years, **Festival de Ballet de La Habana** pays homage to Cuba's ballet culture, with top performances taking place in Havana's major theaters.

December: For cinephiles, **Festival de Nuevo Cine Latinoamericano** showcases the best of Cuban and Latin American cinema, with screenings of new releases.

ACCOMMODATION LOWDOWN

High season means higher accommodation prices, but with literally thousands of casas particulares (private homestays), you'll never struggle to find a place. High-end boutique casas and hotels will need to be booked well in advance.

Getting There

The vast majority of travelers will arrive in Havana by air. Aeropuerto Internacional José Martí is around 20km southwest of Havana.

From the Airport to the City Center

By Taxi

As you leave the airport, you will be bombarded by locals shouting 'taxi!' and it can be a little overwhelming. A standard ride will cost you approximately US$25-30 and take 30 to 40 minutes to reach most places in the city. You are safe to jump into any vehicle but official taxis are yellow and black, and the driver will be dressed smartly.

By Private Transfer

For peace of mind, some like to prebook transport from the airport by organizing a private car. Many hotels and casas can help you organize a convertible classic car with a driver so you can ride into the city in style.

By Shuttle Bus

There is an airport shuttle bus service to and from Terminal 3 that makes multiple stop-offs at the main major hotels in Playa, Vedado and, finally, Habana Vieja. A ride costs US$5 that is normally paid with card (although they sometimes accept cash). Timetables start late morning and finish around midnight, running roughly every hour. However, timings can be unpredictable. Getting a taxi to the airport is the most reliable option so you don't run the risk of missing your flight.

Other Points of Entry

Aeropuerto Internacional José Martí isn't the only place in the country that visitors fly into. Other popular airports are Varadero, Holguín and some of the island's resort cays. After enjoying some beach time, many visit Havana by land, in either a private taxi or bus.

Boats

A very few arrive in Havana via boat, docking in Marina Hemingway (p122) or, occasionally, Havana Bay's cruise-ship port. In 2019, as part of a wave of restrictions, the US banned cruise-ship travel to Cuba, causing the industry in Cuba to plummet.

Getting Around

A lot of Havana is traversable on foot, and it's one of the best ways to explore the city. To get from A to B faster, grab a cab in the street or use one of Cuba's cab-hailing apps or Whatsapp groups such as Muévete *(muevetehabana.com)*. Havana has a very complex public transport system that is worth trying if you want to experience the local way of getting around.

Renting a Car

Car rental in Cuba is expensive and vehicles are in short supply. Cuba has very low car ownership, meaning traffic in Havana is very minimal. However, driving can be stressful given the city's severe potholes, poor signage, one-way streets and obstacles in the road.

Taxi

You're never far from a taxi. Drivers hang around in front of the major tourist hotels, outside the two main bus stations and at various city-center nexus points such as Parque Central (p53) and Parque de la Fraternidad (p83). The most common taxis are the yellow cabs of Cubataxi, which are generally modern, air-conditioned, and fitted with meters – they also cost more. The more battered the vehicle the more of a chance you have to haggle. Always agree on a price before getting into the car. For inner-city travel, taxis are typically paid in Cuban pesos, although many drivers will accept foreign currency.

Tourist Bus

The handy hop-on, hop-off Habana Bus Tour includes the route T3, which runs from Parque Central (p53) to Playas del Este (via Parque Histórico Militar Morro-Cabaña; p132). Buses go every half-hour from 9am to 4:20pm and cost $10 return paid in cash.

Bici-taxis

In Habana Vieja and Centro Habana, you'll be able to find a bici-taxi (rickshaw) on practically every

PORNPRASIT PANADA/SHUTTERSTOCK

ESSENTIAL APP

La Nave is Cuba's answer to Uber but you will need a Cuban phone number to use it.

street corner. This is a great way to get around these areas when you're tired and hot.

Bike

Several reputable companies in Havana hire out bikes that are fine for getting around town. **Chivo** *(Insta: chivo_is_bicycle_in_cuba)*, **Vélo** *(veloencuba.com)* and **Ruta Bikes** (p109) are the best options. If you're uncertain of the geography or the manic road rules, take a guided tour first.

Boat

A passenger ferry crosses the harbor between Habana Vieja's Emboque de Luz, and Casablanca and Regla. This service has become unreliable lately but if you are relaxed for time it is worth it to explore the views from Casablanca and the Afro-Cuban culture of Regla.

Víazul Buses

If you want to head out of the city to other provinces, long-distance bus company Víazul *(viazul.wetransp.com)* is a great way to do so. Tickets can only be paid for with a credit card, or buy in advance on the website (you will need a VPN if you're in Cuba). Services depart from Terminal Omnibus Nacionales close to Plaza de la Revolución.

Public Transport Essentials

- *Máquinas* are shared taxis in old American cars (more ragged-looking than the shiny models you see for tourists in Parque Central). They start and end in Parque Curita (p83) in Centro Habana and finish in Playa, running through Vedado's two main drags: 23 and Línea. Hop in and let the driver know where along the route you want to stop. Journeys should cost less than a dollar in the equivalent of Cuban pesos (drivers won't accept foreign currency).
- *Ruteros* (also known as *gacelas*) are black and yellow minivans that service different routes between districts.
- The cheapest mode of transport is public buses *(guaguas)*, which only cost two pesos, but due to fuel shortages in recent years their services have been reduced, and vehicles are severely overcrowded.

Need to Know

As of 2025, Cuba was experiencing power cuts, fuel shortages and a scarcity of some commodities. Havana is much less affected by blackouts, known as *apagones*, than the rest of the island, but outages are still a daily reality.

Top Tips

- Keep your electronic devices charged whenever there's electricity, as outages can happen randomly and for unspecified periods of time.
- *Apagones* make opening hours volatile. If there's no power, museums, restaurants and clubs can close without warning.
- Bring a power bank, flashlight and a rechargeable hand fan.
- Some generators are not powerful enough to fuel the air-con and wi-fi.
- Habana Vieja is the area that experiences the fewest *apagones* in the city.
- Remember, after years of hardship, the Cubans are experts in improvising and working things out. Casa owners and hotel staff will be able to help you with planning and circumventing issues.

APAGONES

Many hotels, casas particulares and restaurants have generators for when the power goes out, but most budget places do not.

AMERICAN TRAVELERS

Americans have been experiencing restrictions on travel to Cuba since the early 1960s. The only certainty is that official government policies change regularly. Always check ahead. Travel is authorized under 12 self-qualifying categories. Many independent travelers go under the 'support for the Cuban people' category, which stipulates that tourists must engage in activities and frequent places that support Cubans and their private businesses over government-run institutions.

CURRENT RESTRICTIONS

Americans are prohibited from staying in most state-run Cuban hotels – and from dealing with any other state-run businesses.

US cruise ships are prohibited from calling at Cuban ports.

Cuban alcohol and tobacco can not be imported into the US.

US credit cards still don't work in Cuba, so come armed with all the money you'll need in cash.

A Few Surprises

Havana is a city of many layers and secrets that go well beyond classic cars, revolutionary propaganda and smiling salsa musicians.

Treasure Hunting

The cliché of Havana being a city 'trapped in time' holds true when it comes to the old relics that people sell in their front rooms or at local markets. **Feria de Publicaciones y Curiosidades** (p68) in the Antigua Casa de Justiz y Santa Ana is a little-known antiques markets piled high with fascinating trinkets. **Casa Belkis** (p113) is a Vedado home that is disorderedly packed to the rafters with all sorts of antiques.

Boxing & Baseball

Stumble into **Gimnasio de Boxeo Rafael Trejo** (p59) in the gritty San Isidro zone, the apex of Havana's boxing scene is open for shows, training and talent spotting. The national sport is baseball and it's fiercely debated all day, every day at a noisy nexus in **Parque Central** (p53) known as the *esquina caliente* (hot corner).

For a game featuring Havana's beloved Industriales, you'll need to get to the **Estadio Latinoamericano** (Zequiera No 312, Cerro; tickets US$2) in the municipality of Cerro, just as President Obama did when he visited Cuba in March 2016 (the season runs August to January).

Santería Secrets

One of the most practiced faiths in Havana is Santería, a blend of west African Yoruba and European Catholicism originating in Cuba centuries ago. Owing to its African roots, animal sacrifice is an important ritual, so if you see a pig's head or chicken carcass on a downtown street corner you'll know why.

Keep your eyes peeled, particularly in the Afro-Cuban hubs of Centro

OFFBEAT HAVANA

Check out street art of the infamous barrio **San Isidro** (p59) in Habana Vieja, the former stomping ground of Cuba's most iconic pimp.

Dine at the iconic club FAC's rooftop restaurant **Tierra** (p112) which also gets you automatic access to the uber-cool VIP section.

Ask at reception for a free tour of **Hotel Nacional** (p94), including underground nuclear bunkers built during the Cuban Missile Crisis.

Find **Calle Tacón** (p49), or Calle de Madera, a tiny wooden street from the early 1800s which was unearthed in the 1980s.

WANGKUN JIA/SHUTTERSTOCK

Barrio Chino (p81)

Habana, Regla and Guanabacoa for symbols and objects placed in doorways to protect homes. A cactus is believed to offer protection and is hung on doors, while depictions of an eye and a tongue with a knife through it is said to ward off evil energy (known as *mal de ojo*). From time to time, you may see curious objects at the bottom of ceiba trees, or flowers and pumpkins bobbing in rivers and shorelines. These are also part of rituals and offerings associated with Afro-Cuban religions. Don't touch them.

Chinese History

Many are unaware that by the early 20th century, Havana had the largest Asian neighborhood in Latin America. Today, the city's **Barrio Chino** (p81) only feels faintly Chinese, but exploring the area uncovers the residue of its oriental origins. Look for street signs, restaurant names, and plaques written in Chinese and Spanish with the word 'sociedad,' former Chinese societies.

On Calle Zanja, the barrio's main thoroughfare, you will places selling bonsais, Parque Perkin, and a pharmacy selling traditional Chinese medicinal lotions and potions. **Escuela Cubana de Wushu** (p81) is an open-air space that holds martial arts classes. To dig even deeper into this history, visit **Cementerio Chino** (p109), a Chinese cemetery for the Asian immigrant population that settled in the city.

Explore Havana

Top Experiences

Bici-taxi
MAGIC26/SHUTTERSTOCK

See p64 for eating, drinking and shopping listings

Explore Habana Vieja

Havana's Old Town is one of the historical highlights of Latin America; an architectural masterpiece where fastidiously preserved squares and grandiose palaces sit alongside a living, breathing urban community still emerging from decades of economic austerity. The result is by turns grand and gritty. No one should leave Cuba without seeing it. Start by visiting the restored center, including four spectacular squares and several historic hotels. Wander down two of Habana Vieja's most famous streets, the bustling Obispo and the cobbled Mercaderes. Then venture away from the pristine part of town into San Isidro, a raw and real glimpse at a typical inner-city neighborhood with a notorious history.

Getting Around

Bici-taxi

Cycle rickshaws are everywhere you look in Habana Vieja. If you're tired of walking, jump in one and let them peddle you to your destination.

Boat

Small passenger ferries run to Casablanca and Regla on the eastern side of Havana's harbor.

Taxi

Grab a taxi from Parque Central, but remember: they will inflate prices so get ready to do some haggling!

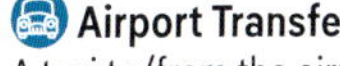

Airport Transfer

A taxi to/from the airport from Habana Vieja takes around 40 minutes.

THE BEST

ARCHITECTURAL WONDER Plaza Vieja (p42)

HISTORIC STREET Calle Mercaderes (p50)

BAROQUE CHURCH Catedral de la Habana (p44)

NATIONAL ART GALLERY Museo Nacional de Bellas Artes (p54)

PEOPLE WATCHING Plaza del Cristo (p58)

Calle Obispo (p52)

WANGKUN JIA/SHUTTERSTOCK

For more see
Top Experiences p42
Experiences p58
Eating p64
Drinking p66
Shopping p67
0 200 m
0 0.1 miles
Bahía de la Habana
Parque de los Enamorados
Museo Nacional de la Música
Parque Mártires del 71
Callejón de los Peluqueros
Parque Anfiteatro
Av Carlos Manuel de Céspedes
Parque Luz Caballero
Catedral de la Habana
Plaza 13 de Marzo
Plazuela de Santo Ángel
Museo de la Revolución
Escuela Nacional de Ballet
LOMA DEL ÁNGEL
Casa del Mayorazgo Recio
Castillo de la Real Fuerza
Plaza de la Catedral
Palacio del Segundo Cabo
Museo El Templete
Calle Tacón
Plaza de Armas
Museo Universitario
Museo de la Ciudad
See Calle Mercaderes
La Casona del Son
Museo Nacional de Bellas Artes
Sloppy Joe's
Edificio Bacardí
Calle Obispo
Banco Nacional de Cuba
Libreria Fayad Jamis
Hotel Iberostar Parque Central
Gran Hotel Manzana Kempinski
El Ojo del Ciclón
HABANA VIEJA
Hostal Conde de Villanueva
Edificio Lonja del Comercio
Parque Central
Gran Teatro de la Habana Alicia Alonso
Museo Nacional de Bellas Artes-Arte Universal
Museo del Automóvil
Hotel Raquel
Basílica Menor de San Francisco de Asís
Plaza de San Francisco de Asís
Consulado
Genios
Paseo de Martí (Prado)
Refugio
Colón
Trocadero
Ánimas
Virtudes
Habana
Aguiar
Cuba
Tacón
Cuarteles
Chacón
Tejadillo
Empedrado
San Ignacio
O'Reilly
San Juan de Dios
Villegas
Obispo
Aguacate
Compostela
Bernaza
Lamparilla
Amargura
Mercaderes
Oficios
Obrapía
Baratillo
Jústiz

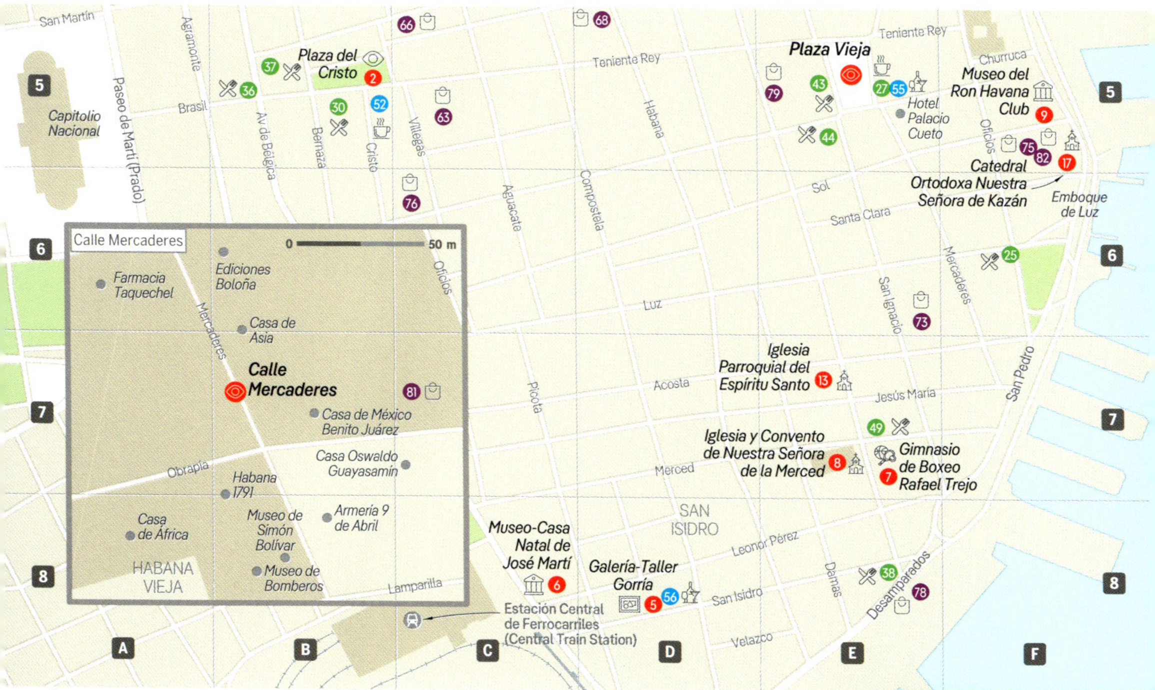

Plaza del Cristo

Plaza Vieja

Museo del Ron Havana Club

Hotel Palacio Cueto

Catedral Ortodoxa Nuestra Señora de Kazán

Emboque de Luz

Capitolio Nacional

Calle Mercaderes

0 — 50 m

Farmacia Taquechel

Ediciones Boloña

Casa de Asia

Calle Mercaderes

Casa de México Benito Juárez

Casa Oswaldo Guayasamín

Habana 1791

Casa de África

Museo de Simón Bolívar

Armería 9 de Abril

Museo de Bomberos

HABANA VIEJA

Iglesia Parroquial del Espíritu Santo

Iglesia y Convento de Nuestra Señora de la Merced

Gimnasio de Boxeo Rafael Trejo

SAN ISIDRO

Museo-Casa Natal de José Martí

Galería-Taller Gorría

Estación Central de Ferrocarriles (Central Train Station)

San Martín, Agramonte, Paseo de Martí (Prado), Brasil, Av de Bélgica, Bernaza, Cristo, Villegas, Aguacate, Compostela, Habana, Teniente Rey, Churruca, Oficios, Sol, Santa Clara, Luz, Mercaderes, San Ignacio, Acosta, Jesús María, Picota, Merced, Obrapía, Lamparilla, Leonor Pérez, Damas, San Isidro, Desamparados, Velazco, San Pedro

★ TOP EXPERIENCE

Plaza Vieja

Its name is deceptive, as Plaza Vieja (Old Square) is not the oldest in Habana Vieja but the third to be developed. Laid out in 1559, Plaza Vieja is Havana's most architecturally eclectic plaza, where Cuban baroque nestles seamlessly next to Gaudí-inspired art nouveau.

MAP P40 **E5**

PLANNING TIP
Other attractions on the square worth a look include a camera obscura and a planetarium. Look out on the western side of Plaza Vieja for some of Havana's finest *vitrales* (stained-glass windows) adorning the upper floors.

The Plaza's Palaces

Originally called Plaza Nueva (New Square), it was used for military exercises and later served as an open-air marketplace. Unlike other squares, Plaza Vieja is purely residential. The distinctive **Hotel Palacio Cueto**, at the southeastern corner of the square, is Havana's finest example of art nouveau. Its ornate facade, dating from 1906, once fronted a warehouse and a hat factory before the building was rented by José Cueto in the 1920s as the Palacio Vienna hotel. At the square's south-western corner, **Palacio de los Condes de Jaruco** was constructed in 1738 from local limestone in a transitional Mudéjar baroque style. This muscular mansion is one of Plaza Vieja's oldest. Rich in period detail, it is typical of merchant houses of the era. For many years it was the residence of the exalted counts of Jaruco. Today it's the headquarters of Cuba's main cultural foundation. It underwent a lengthy restoration in the early 2020s.

El Gallo

South of the square is an eye-catching sculpture of a naked woman riding a cockerel, wielding a giant fork. Created by artist Roberto Fabelo in 2004 and installed in the plaza in 2013, the rooster is an

MAURIZIO DE MATTEI/SHUTTERSTOCK

important symbol of strength and masculinity in Cuban and wider Latino culture, but the woman on top of the majestic bronze bird, taming the feathered beast, represents female empowerment.

The Fountain

A fountain has anchored the square since the 18th century and was originally fashioned in Carrara marble by Italian sculptor Giorgio Massari. It was (shamefully) demolished in the 1950s to make way for an underground car park, but a replica of the fountain was installed in the early 2010s. For a while it was surrounded by a black fence, supposedly to stop local schoolchildren jumping in it. The fence has been removed and the kids still play rambunctiously nearby.

TAKE A BREAK
Plaza Vieja is a decent eating and drinking option; head under the arches to Café Bohemia (p65) or to the always-lively iconic restaurant La Vitrola (p65).

★ TOP EXPERIENCE

Catedral de la Habana

Designed by Italian architect Francesco Borromini, Havana's incredible cathedral was once described by novelist Alejo Carpentier as 'music set in stone.' The Jesuits began construction of the church in 1748 and work continued despite their expulsion in 1767. The church was finally consecrated in 1789.

MAP P40 **D2**

PLANNING TIP
Dress appropriately for the church: no sleeveless tops or micro-shorts. Return to the square at night, when it has a totally different (and more intimate) atmosphere.

Scan the QR code for opening hours and mass times.

Front Facade

The cathedral's unusual swirling facade is considered to be the apex of baroque architecture in Cuba. Although visually arresting and unique,

the exterior walls were not as lavishly decorated as those of similar churches in Europe. This is due primarily to the hardness of the local limestone, but the lack of skilled craftspeople in 18th-century Cuba also played a role. Look closely and you'll see marine fossils embedded in the walls and pillars.

TAKE A BREAK
One of the finest exponents of traditional Cuban food, Doña Eutimia (p64) is located in a cul-de-sac just off the square. Also close by is the lively Fonda al Pirata (p64).

Interior

In contrast to its ornate facade, the cathedral's interior is neoclassical rather than baroque and relatively austere, the result of puritanical remodeling by an early-19th-century bishop. There are original Italian frescoes above the altar; the less valuable oil canvases that adorn the side walls are copies of works by Bartolomé Esteban Murillo and Peter Paul Rubens. You can climb the smaller of the cathedral's towers for a small fee.

MAGIC26/SHUTTERSTOCK

★ TOP EXPERIENCE

Plaza de San Francisco de Asís

Facing Havana harbor, this breezy plaza first grew up in the 16th century when Spanish galleons stopped quayside on their passage from the Caribbean to Spain. A market took root in the 1500s, followed by a church in 1608, though when the monks complained about noise, the market was moved to Plaza Vieja.

MAP P40 **F4**

PLANNING TIP
Basílica Menor de San Francisco de Asís typically holds classical music recitals every Saturday late afternoon, although timetables are irregular.

Scan this QR code to see upcoming concerts in the plaza's church.

Pigeon Park

In 1761 this plaza, also known as Pigeon Park or Plaza de las Palomas, was surrounded by the city hall, police house, jailhouse and the customs office. Today, dotted around the cobbled plaza are three historic five-star hotels, a deconsecrated church and the **Lonja del Comercio**, Havana's former stock exchange. With an eclectic style and Renaissance decoration, this was the city's first building with an elevator.

Basílica Menor de San Francisco de Asís

This former Franciscan **convent** was constructed between 1575 and 1591 and is now a concert hall. In front stands the white-marble Fuente de los Leones, a fountain carved by Italian sculptor Giuseppe Gaggini in 1836.

Statues

El Caballero de París is the plaza's most famous statue. It's a realistic depiction of a well-known street person who roamed Havana during the 1950s, engaging passersby with his philosophies on life, religion and politics. It is seen as good luck to touch his beard, which is why that part of the statue has turned color from bronze to gold. Similarly, **La Conversación** is a modernist bronze rendition by French artist Étienne of two seated people talking.

★ TOP EXPERIENCE

Plaza de Armas

Havana's oldest square was laid out in the early 1520s, established soon after the founding of Havana in 1519. Today, this plaza, with its impressive baroque facades, harbors some of Havana's best museums, an iconic hotel, and a beautiful garden in the center with statues and stunning greenery.

MAP P40 **E3**

Museo de la Ciudad

Even with no artifacts, Havana's city museum would be a tour de force, courtesy of the opulent palace in which it resides. Filling the whole western side of Plaza de Armas, **Palacio de los Capitanes Generales** (pictured p47) dates from the 1770s and is a textbook example of Cuban baroque, hewn out of rock from the nearby San Lázaro quarries. Huge rooms guard equally huge exhibits. From 1791 until 1898 the palace was the residence of the Spanish 'captains general,' the colony's administrative rulers. Then, for a brief period between 1899 and 1902, US military governors were based here. During the first two decades of the 20th century the building briefly became the presidential palace and, later, Havana's City Hall. The museum was created in 1968 after the palace became one of the first buildings in Habana Vieja to be renovated by Eusebio Leal, the City Historian.

The site on which the museum now stands was once occupied by Havana's main church, Iglesia Mayor Parroquial de La Habana, built in the 1550s. The church was severely damaged when a ship blew up in Havana harbor in 1741 and was never repaired. Ultimately replaced by Havana's new Jesuit-built cathedral, it was finally demolished in

PLANNING TIP
Spare some time to visit the opulent Segundo Cabo building on the north side of Plaza de Armas, a museum dedicated to Cuban-European cultural relations.

Scan this QR code for admission details for Museo de la Ciudad.

DIANA RITA CABRERA/LONELY PLANET

1771 to make way for the current palace. The museum contains collections of objects and vessels rescued from the original building.

The museum is regally wrapped around a splendid central courtyard adorned with a white-marble statue of Christopher Columbus (1862). Its artifacts (some of them a tad dusty) include period furniture, military uniforms and antique horse carriages. The real history-defining highlights are the boat used by Antonio Maceo to cross the Trocha de Mariel in 1896, a cannon captured from the Spanish by soldiers during the Independence War in 1897, and Cuba's first flag, raised by Narciso López in Cárdenas in 1850.

TAKE A BREAK
Nip up Calle O'Reilly for some cocktails and tapas at the ever-popular rooftop bar and restaurant El del Frente (p67).

Hotel Santa Isabel

This hotel was once the palatial residence of the counts of Santovenia. With elegant arches and sky-blue wooden shutters, the strapping baroque beauty first opened as a hotel in 1867. Its long list of esteemed guests includes former US president Jimmy Carter.

Castillo de la Real Fuerza

Castillo de la real Fuerza is one of the oldest surviving forts in the Americas, built from 1558 and completed in 1577 to defend against pirates. It replaced the former fort Fuerza Vieja that was damaged during an attack and was deemed to be too set back from the harbor. However, the location of this new structure eventually was also determined to be too far away from the seafront and it was turned into the residence of the Governor of Havana.

Museo El Templete

Construction of this important monument, whose design was inspired by a Greek temple, began in 1827 to commemorate the founding of Havana on November 16, 1519. Museo El Templete was built on this site as it was said to be where the first mass and town council meeting were held, under the shade of a nearby ceiba tree. Since then, it has become a tradition every November 16 for Cubans to pilgrimage to the site, walk three times anti-clockwise around the ceiba to make a wish and to leave offerings at the foot of its trunk. In the middle of the 18th century the tree died, and it has been replaced several times, the last being in 2016.

Calle de Madera

Unique to this plaza is Calle Tacón, a tiny strip of street made from wooden paving dating back to the early 1800s. This gem was uncovered in the 1980s when restoration of Old Havana began.

HEMINGWAY HAUNT

A block away from the plaza is **Hotel Ambos Mundos**, where the great American writer famously lived for seven years in the 1930s. Head to the rooftop for a drink and some great views.

★ TOP EXPERIENCE

Calle Mercaderes

Cobbled, car-free Calle Mercaderes (Merchants' Street) has been extensively restored by the Office of the City Historian and is an almost complete replica of itself at its splendid 18th-century high-water mark. Interspersed with the museums, shops and restaurants are some working social projects, such as a maternity home and a paper-making cooperative.

MAP P40 **B7**

PLANNING TIP
Check out the small bookshop **Boloña**, on the corner of Mercaderes and Obispo, that sells books, mostly in Spanish, that track the astounding renovation of Habana Vieja, illustrated with excellent photos.

Free Museums

Most of the myriad museums are free, including **Casa de Asia** (pictured right), with paintings and sculpture from China and Japan, as well as an oriental-inspired patio garden; **Armería 9 de Abril**, an old gun shop (now museum) stormed by revolutionaries on the said date in 1958; and **Museo de Bomberos**, which has antediluvian fire equipment dedicated to 19 Havana firefighters who lost their lives in an 1890 railway blaze.

Casa de África

Just off Mercaderes down Obrapía, it's worth slinking into the gratis Casa de África, which houses sacred objects relating to Santería and the secret Abakuá fraternity collected by ethnographer Fernando Ortiz.

An International Flavor

The corner of Mercaderes and Obrapía has an international theme, with a bronze statue of Latin America liberator Simón Bolívar; across the street you'll find **Museo de Simón Bolívar**, dedicated to Bolívar's life. **Casa de México Benito Juárez** exhibits Mexican folk art and plenty of books but not a lot on Juárez (Mexico's first indigenous

WANGKUN JIA/SHUTTERSTOCK

president) himself. Just east is **Casa Oswaldo Guayasamín**, now a museum but once the studio of the great Ecuadorian artist who painted Fidel Castro in numerous poses.

Shops

Mercaderes is characterized by its restored shops, including a specialist perfume store, museum and laboratory, **Habana 1791**. Perfumes arrived at the city's port from Europe from the 17th century, and the fragrances sold here are an ode to colonial Havana: tobacco, rose, violet and sandalwood. You can mix your own blends and purchase special personalized flasks and vials. There is also a spice shop, and a chocolate 'museum' that sells the sweet stuff out of an alluring streetside window on the corner of Amargura (bitterness) Street. One of the city's best tobacco stores is encased in the beautifully reimagined **Hostal Conde de Villanueva**. Wander at will.

TAKE A BREAK
One of Havana's top restaurants is the elegant Paladar Los Mercaderes (p66). Sit on one of the little balconies to see the action of Calle Mercaderes below.

★ TOP EXPERIENCE

Calle Obispo

Narrow, chockablock Calle Obispo (Bishop's St), Habana Vieja's main interconnecting artery, is packed with art galleries, shops, music venues and people. This crowded thoroughfare provides an immersive introduction to the city's moods and rhythms.

MAP P40 **D3**

TAKE A BREAK
There are many eating and drinking spots to choose from along Obispo, including tourist bar **La Lluvia de Oro** with live Cuban music and La Caribeña (p64), which offers decent and well-priced Cuban food.

Tourists & Locals Collide

Brimming with both Cuban and tourist activity, this street can be an overwhelming experience, as locals compete to lure you into nearby restaurants and spark up a conversation. That being said, there are people from all walks of life parading up and down this street, and it's great for people watching. Pop into Feria de Obispo (p68), a bustling market where you can buy touristy bits and pieces, while **Librería Fayad Jamis** is a bookstore with a variety of interesting reads in English and Spanish.

Obispo's Businesses

There are a broad range of businesses, from shabby-looking state-run sites to interesting private enterprises, as well as specialist museums, bookshops, art galleries and the ostentatious **Farmacia Taquechel**. The pharmacy's elegant chandeliers and long lines of ceramic jars evoke times past. The Mudéjar-style **Casa del Mayorazgo Recio**, near the corner of Mercaderes, is Havana's oldest building.

Cuba's Wall Street

Several magnificent old banks from Havana's former days of economic prosperity have now become government buildings and museums. The **Banco Nacional de Cuba**, on Obispo and Calle Cuba, was erected in 1907 and is now the headquarters of the Ministry of Finance and Prices.

★ TOP EXPERIENCE

Parque Central

This hyperactive square, which marks the official city center, sits on the cusp of Old and Centro Havana and is distinguished by its priest-like statue of José Martí, Cuba's national hero, rendered in Carrara marble and surrounded by 28 palm trees, representing his birthday (January 28, 1853).

MAP P40 **A4**

Havana Hotels

The park is ringed by some of Havana's most illustrious hotels. **Iberostar Parque Central** has a huge, loungey lobby and an elegant rooftop pool. The five-star **Kempinski** sits atop the Manzana de Gómez, an early-20th-century European-style shopping mall. Head to its swanky rooftop to sip a cocktail and take a selfie against the dramatic backdrop of El Capitolio. On the other side of the park is Hotel Inglaterra (p84), Havana's oldest hotel.

Esquina Caliente

Follow the shouts emanating from the omnipresent group of men who stand arguing near the José Martí statue. The topic is generally baseball and the melee is known as the *esquina caliente* ('hot corner'), after the corner of Calles 23 and 12 in Vedado where it originally convened.

Gran Teatro de la Habana Alicia Alonso

The neobaroque theater is named after the world-famous Cuban prima ballerina. The site was first erected as a Galician social club between 1907 and 1914, and features highly ornate architectural details. It's the official stage for the Cuban National Ballet Company and the headquarters of the biennial International Ballet Festival. At the time of research, the theater was closed for renovations.

PLANNING TIP

Parque Central is a great transport hub for taking a city tour in a classic car, a bus to the beach, or a taxi across town. For taxis, make sure you negotiate hard on the price.

Scan this QR code to book specialized classic car tours with Havana Super Tour.

★ TOP EXPERIENCE

Museo Nacional de Bellas Artes

Spread over two campuses, Bellas Artes is arguably the finest art gallery in the Caribbean. The **Arte Cubano** building contains an impressive and comprehensive collection of Cuban art, while the **Arte Universal** section is laid out in a grand eclectic palace overlooking Parque Central.

MAP P40 **B3**

PLANNING TIP
If you're short on time, focus on the Arte Cubano collection. If you want to see both, set aside a good 90 minutes for each museum.

Scan this QR code to visit the website and see what exhibitions are on.

Arte Cubano Collection

The Cuban collection is exhibited in the original museum building on Trocadero, between Agramonte and Av de las Misiones, which dates from 1955. Works are displayed in chronological order, starting on the 3rd floor, and are surprisingly varied. Artists to look out for include Guillermo Collazo, considered to be the first truly great Cuban artist; Rafael Blanco, with his cartoon-like paintings and sketches; Raúl Martínez, a master of 1960s Cuban pop art; and Wifredo Lam.

Lam was an avant-garde painter and sculptor of Chinese, African and Spanish ancestry who studied in Havana before departing for Europe in 1923, gravitating to Spain and later France, where he became friends with Pablo Picasso. Mixing cubist and surrealist influences with the diverse motifs of his Cuban heritage (especially Santería), he produced his masterpiece, *La Jungla*, in 1943. Although this painting isn't currently displayed in Bellas Artes, there are many other of his works there.

Arte Universal Collection

Since 2001 the international collection, displaying art from 500 BCE to the present day, has been exhibited on three floors of the Palacio de los Asturianos, located on San Rafael between

ROBERTO LA ROSA/ALAMY

Agramonte and Av de las Misiones. Its undisputed highlight is its Spanish collection, with canvases by Francisco de Zurbarán, Bartolomé Esteban Murillo and Jusepe de Ribera, and a tiny work by Diego Velázquez. Also worth perusing are the 2000-year-old Roman mosaics, Greek pots from the 5th century BCE, and a suitably refined canvas by Thomas Gainsborough (in the British room).

La Gitana Tropical

Sometimes dubbed the 'Mona Lisa of the Caribbean,' this simple but haunting study of a woman by Havana-born painter Víctor Manuel García Valdés was executed in Paris in 1929 and shows distinct European influences. Valdés was part of the Vanguardia movement of artists and his *Gitana* isn't just the country's most cherished painting but also serves as a precursor to Cuban modernism.

QUICK BREAK

There are two top restaurants close to Bellas Artes; ChaChaChá (p66), with a variety of Cuban and international fare, and Al Carbón (p65), owned by the former chef of Fidel Castro.

WALKING TOUR

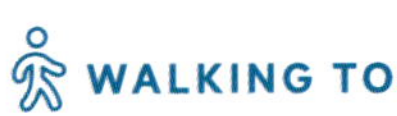

Rehabilitated Habana

The piecing together of Habana Vieja began in the late 1970s and is ongoing. The project, run by the Office of the City Historian, has restored Havana's most important historic buildings, created groundbreaking social projects for the local population, and garnered numerous international prizes for its cultural, historical and sustainable work.

START	END	LENGTH
Plaza de Armas	Galería-Taller Gorría	2km; one to two hours

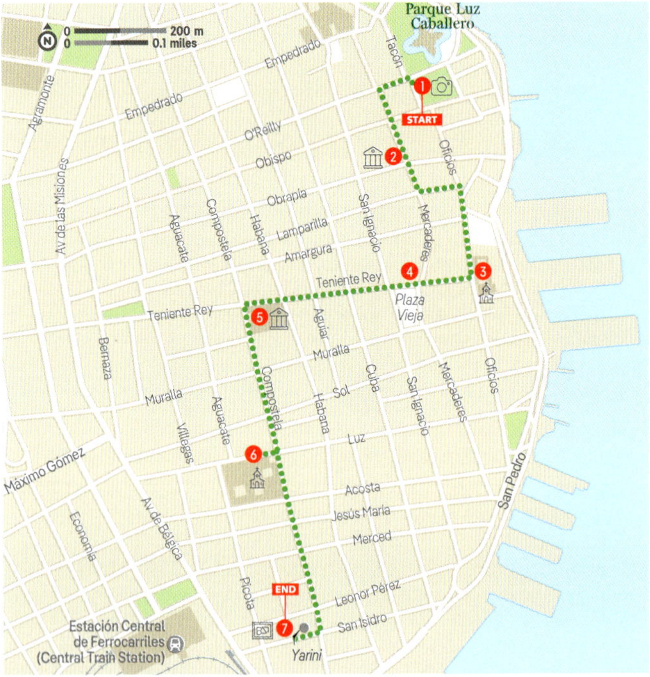

1 Plant-filled Plaza

Plaza de Armas (p47), the oldest spot in Habana Vieja, is simply beautiful and stunningly restored. The inner garden is an urban oasis of greenery, palm trees and grand statues that is a joy to wander through. The square is surrounded by museums, forts and other points of interest.

2 Spanish Nostalgia

An architectural highlight in Habana Vieja is the **Casa de la Obra Pía**, originally a Spanish nobleman's mansion. The house was rehabilitated in 1983 as a museum and community project. The rooms facing Calle Mercaderes usually host revolving art exhibitions.

3 Musical Monastery

Built in 1608, Iglesia y Monasterio de San Francisco de Asís ceased to have a religious function in the 1840s. Crypts and religious objects were dug up during excavations in the 1980s, and many of them are contained in the **Museo de Arte Religioso** that opened on the site in 1994.

4 Local Life

Plaza Vieja (p42) is perhaps the City Historian's most beautifully restored square, but it's not all for tourists. On its northern side is the Angela Landa school, which occasionally uses the square as substitute playground and alfresco classroom. You'll see students running, playing sports, or sitting and reading beneath the giant *portales* (galleried walkways).

5 Pharmacy Museum

The wonderful art nouveau Sarrá pharmacy was founded by a Catalan immigrant in 1888. Restored in the 1990s, it functions as a **Museo de la Farmacia Habanera** and a working pharmacy for the local population, selling mainly homeopathic products.

6 Repurposed Church

The huge 18th-century **Iglesia y Convento de Nuestra Señora de Belén** was restored by the City Historian in the 1990s, turning the building into an active community center. There are 18 permanent apartments for seniors, plus a sporadically open meteorology museum.

7 Urban Art Project

The grid of streets south of Calle Acosta was designated a special **art district** in the mid-2010s, with murals, galleries and regular events inspired by a mix of entrepreneurs and the Office of the City Historian. Center of operations is the Galería-Taller Gorría (p59), owned by Cuban actor Jorge Perugorría and the affiliated bar/restaurant Yarini (p67).

EXPERIENCES

Sip Coffee in Plazuela de Santo Ángel

PLAZA

MAP: 1 P40 **B2**

This lovely, intimate plaza behind the Iglesia del Santo Ángel Custodio has benefited from a community-driven beautification project that has installed several private restaurants, along with a statue of the fictional heroine Cecilia Valdés, who is watched over by a bust of the author who created her, Cirilo Villaverde.

People Watch in Plaza del Cristo

PLAZA

MAP: 2 P40 **B5**

A little apart from the historical core, Plaza del Cristo hasn't benefited from a full restoration yet and this adds subtly to its charm. Here you can sidestep boisterous games of football, chill out at several cool bars, or browse a few cutting-edge private businesses.

Wander Down Hairdressers' Alley

STREET

MAP: 3 P40 **C1**

The brainchild of barber Gilberto Valladares, aka 'Papito,' this revitalized community project is based upon a novel hairdressing salon that doubles up as a school and small museum to the barber's art. With a little help from some his friends and Havana's City Historian, Papito's barber theme has taken over the whole street, now rechristened **Callejón de los Peluqueros** and supported by more than 20 independent businesses.

Museo Universitario

MUSEUM

MAP: 4 P40 **E3**

This expertly curated museum tells the story of the numerous institutions that once stood on this site on Calle Mercaderes, from the erstwhile Convento de San Juan de Letrán, established in 1570, to the Dominican-run University of Havana, which welcomed students

COOKING WITH LA LORE

Learn from the best by taking a cooking class from a Cuban TV chef. Lorena (@laloreestacocinando) hosts a cooking channel on national television and has developed her own in-person experience for visitors wanting to learn how to make home-cooked Cuban food. Lorena teaches you how to make typical Cuban starters such as malanga fritters, mains such as the national dish, *ropa vieja*, and cocktails. Throughout, she shares fascinating facts and backstories to these dishes that you won't easily find on Google. This class takes place on the rooftop open kitchen of her beautiful Old Havana casa particular.

between 1728 and 1902 before moving to Vedado. The contemporary building was constructed over the skeleton of an ugly 1950s office block.

Explore Old Havana's Notorious Neighborhood

STREET ART

MAP: 5 P40 **D8**

A fair walk south from the main action of Habana Vieja you'll find **San Isidro**, a gritty district of the city with a wealth of dark history. Situated between the train terminal and the port, in the early 20th century it was somewhat of a red-light district in Havana, led by an iconic pimp named Alberto Yarini. San Isidro is also a creative hub, where many of its dilapidated streets have been given a fresh lick of paint from Havana's top graffiti artists. The district's unofficial HQ is **Galería-Taller Gorría**, owned by renowned Cuban actor and artist Jorge Perugorría. Next door and marked by a bright neon hat, is the rooftop bar-restaurant aptly named Yarini (p67). San Isidro was also the home of the Movimiento San Isidro (MSI), founded in 2018 to fight censorship in the arts that has since disbanded due to its members being arrested or fleeing the country.

Visit the Birthplace of Cuba's Hero

MUSEUM

MAP: 6 P40 **C8**

Museo-Casa Natal de José Martí, opened in 1925, is set in the house where the apostle of Cuban independence was born on January 28, 1853. The Office of the City Historian took the house over in 1994, and its succinct stash of exhibits devoted to Cuba's national hero continues to impress.

JIBARO FOOD EXPERIENCE

Restaurant **Jibaro** (p66) puts on one of the best foodie experiences in the city. It starts by going food shopping local style in two working-class neighborhoods in Habana Vieja (San Isidro and Jesús María), and visiting two types of markets to learn about how *habaneros* buy and barter their produce. Their expert guide will give you the lowdown on the complexity of shopping in Cuba, including the country's ration system, state vs private businesses and other interesting facts surrounding Cuban daily life. The experience finishes with a mojito-making class at Jibaro and a Cuban lunch.

Sit in on a Cuban Sparring Session

SPORTS GYM

MAP: 7 P40 **E7**

Gimnasio de Boxeo Rafael Trejo is the place to go to see some youngsters battling it out in the ring. Turn up during the week (late afternoons are better) to this gritty boxing gym and see all levels and all ages practicing their fighting skills. You may even be encouraged to step in the ring yourself.

Visit Havana's Most Underrated Church

CHURCH

MAP: 8 P40 E7

Bizarrely overlooked by the tourist hordes, this baroque church, **Iglesia y Convento de Nuestra Señora de la Merced**, in its own small square, has Havana's most sumptuous ecclesiastical interior, only partially restored. Beautiful gilded altars, frescoed vaults and a number of valuable old paintings create a sacrosanct mood. There's a quiet cloister adjacent.

Educate Yourself on Cuba's Favorite Drink

MUSEUM

MAP: 9 P40 F5

Museo del Ron Havana Club *(havanaclubmuseum.com/en)* gives a whistlestop tour of the history of Cuban rum from cane to *copa* (glass). This 45-minute visit, available in English, Spanish, French and German, includes a scale model of a rum factory, profiles of Cuba's highly trained master distillers known as 'maestros,' copious barrels and distillers, and an array of Havana Club bottles, from cheap cocktail mixers to thousand-dollar 'máximos.' There are tours with different pricing tiers which include rum tastings, ranging from a try of a couple of the most classic Havana Club rums to the 'Experiencia Única' package, which includes tasting some of the most prestigious rums and being able to mix, bottle and personalize your very own rum blend to take home. The tour ends at the next-door bar where you can sip a Havana Club–based cocktail.

Explore Colonial Castles

CASTLE

MAP: 10 P40 A1

One in a quartet of forts defending Havana harbor, **Castillo de San Salvador de la Punta** was designed by Italian military engineer Bautista Antonelli and built between 1589 and 1600. It underwent comprehensive repairs after the British shelled it during their successful 1762 Havana raid. In the colonial era a chain was stretched 250m to the castle of El Morro every night to close the harbor mouth to shipping.

The History Behind Cuba's Cars

MUSEUM

MAP: 11 P40 E4

Museo del Automóvil on Calle Ignacio is a great site to explore the automotive history of Cuba. Dozens of vintage vehicles are parked in this former 1891 warehouse also called 'El Garaje' (the garage), all from different periods, dating back as early as a Ford from 1914. The museum also contains a restored 1959 mint green Oldsmobile once owned by Camilo Cienfuegos and a 1977 Ducati 900SS motorcycle allegedly used by Cuban revolutionary Fidel Castro. In 1958, Cuba was sixth in the world in the number of vehicles per capita. Today, the country has the lowest car ownership in Latin America.

Relive the Castro Era at Museo de la Revolución MUSEUM

MAP: 12 P40 **B2**

Cuba's former presidential palace, first occupied by the nation's third president Mario Menocal in 1920, harbors an exhaustive history museum whose exhibits tell a comprehensive, if unashamedly propagandist, story of Cuba's past, with a big focus on events post-1959. The setting is more inspiring. The palace itself is an eclectic masterpiece with an interior furnished by the world-famous Tiffany's of New York. At the time of research, Museo de la Revolución was undergoing an interminable renovation with only the outdoor Pavillón Granma open. The alfresco area contains a replica of the yacht that carried Castro and 81 other revolutionaries from Mexico to Cuba in 1956 along with other vehicles associated with the revolution, including planes, rockets and a postal van used as a getaway vehicle during a 1957 attack.

Feel the Holy Spirit CHURCH

MAP: 13 P40 **E7**

Havana's oldest surviving church, **Iglesia Parroquial del Espíritu Santo**, has been remodeled since its founding as a hermitage, built by freed formerly enslaved black people in 1638. Most of the current edifice dates from the mid-19th century and has Moorish, Gothic, neoclassical and Andalusian styles.

Marvel at Hotel Raquel HISTORIC HOTEL

MAP: 14 P40 **E4**

This hotel *(hotelraquel-cuba.com)* is a shining example of Habana Vieja's ambitious restoration project. Built in 1904, this architectural gem is a mix of Baroque exterior and art nouveau interiors with highly flamboyant and intricate details.

Check Out Surrealist Art ART GALLERY

MAP: 15 P40 **B4**

Just when you think you've seen Havana's strangest, most surreal and avant-garde art, along comes the 'eye of the cyclone' to re-stretch your imagination. The abstract gallery **El Ojo del Ciclón** is the work of Cuban artist Leo D'Lázaro and it's pretty mind-bending stuff – giant eyes, crashed cars, painted suitcases and junk reborn as art. Imagine Jackson Pollock sitting down for tea with JRR Tolkien and John Lennon.

Take in the Beautiful Barcardi Building HISTORIC BUILDING

MAP: 16 P40 **B3**

Completed in 1930, the magnificent **Edificio Bacardí**, once the HQ of Cuba's erstwhile rum dynasty, is a triumph of art deco architecture, with a host of lavish finishes utilizing red granite, green marble, terra-cotta reliefs and glazed tiles. Though 12 stories high, it's hemmed in by other buildings these days, so it's hard to get a panoramic view of the structure from street level. That notwithstanding, the opulent bell tower can be glimpsed from all over Havana.

Ogle at the Orthodox CHURCH

MAP: 17 P40 **F5**

A brilliant white and gold oddity among the rest of Habana Vieja's architecture, this Russian Orthodox church, **Nuestra Señora de Kazán**, was a collaboration between Havana's Historian's Office and Russian architects. The church, built in the early 2000s, has six gold and bronze-plated domes adorned with crosses and is a dramatic addition to Havana's harborside.

Dance at La Casona del Son DANCE SCHOOL

MAP: 18 P40 **C3**

Havana's number one salsa school welcomes dancers of all levels, from the two left-footed to the pros, and teaches all types of Cuban dance, including salsa, rumba, chachacha, rueda de casino and folkloric. The teachers at La Casona del Son are professional but fun and relaxed (and sometimes cheeky!). They also offer percussion music classes as well as Spanish lessons.

Sit at the Bar at Sloppy Joe's HISTORIC BAR

MAP: 19 P40 **A3**

Opened by young Spanish immigrant José García (aka 'Joe') in 1919, Sloppy Joe's earned its name for its dodgy sanitation and soggy *ropa vieja* sandwich. Legendary among expats before the revolution, it closed in the '60s after a fire but was reincarnated in 2013 behind the same noble neoclassical

HISTORICAL JIGSAW

Never in the field of architectural preservation has so much been achieved by so many with so few resources. A work in progress since the late 1970s, the piecing back together of Havana's Old Town after decades of neglect has been a miraculous process, considering the economic odds stacked against it. The genius behind the project was Eusebio Leal Spengler (1942–2020), Havana's late City Historian, who eschewed the temptation to turn Havana's old quarter into a historical theme park and sought to rebuild the city's urban jigsaw as an authentic 'living' center that provides tangible benefits for the neighborhood's 82,000-plus inhabitants.

facade. And it's still serving decent cocktails and soggy sandwiches.

Havana's Ballet Building

DANCE SCHOOL

MAP: 20 P40 **A2**

The **Escuela Nacional de Ballet** *(facebook.com/ENBalletCuba)*, located on the iconic Paseo del Prado (p77), is the world's largest ballet school, with around 3000 students who undergo rigorous training and whose alumni include prima ballerina Alicia Alonso who developed the unique Cuban ballet style. In keeping with Cuba's socialist model, the school is free to attend.

Meander through the National Music Museum

MUSEUM

MAP: 21 P40 **B1**

After being closed for 18 years, undergoing restoration, **Museo Nacional de la Música** *(facebook .com/MuseoNacionaldelaMusica .Cub)* reopened its opulent doors in January 2025. This is perhaps one of the most comprehensive museums in Cuba, tracking the evolution of Cuban music from its indigenous roots to today. It tackles Cuba's most well-known genres, such as salsa, jazz and *son*, but dives into lesser-known musical forms like the centuries-old *el nengón y el kiribá* that originated in the east of the island and *punto Cubano* countryside music. It also features hundreds of musical relics, such as a highly decorative piano owned by Cuban singer and pianist icon Bola de Nieve, phonographs, vinyls and instruments with African origins. The museum has a lot of information, so using a guide is advisable, although there are currently none available in English.

BEST BREAKFASTS

El Café

Tight service, exceptional coffee and homemade sourdough sandwiches supplemented by all-day brunchy breakfasts. This place is rightly popular with indie travelers courtesy of its ample vegan and vegetarian options. (p64)

La Vitrola

A retro '50s nook on the corner of Plaza Vieja, La Vitrola offers quiet alfresco breakfasts of fruit, coffee, toast, and generous omelets, which come complete with a toothpick flag of your home country. (p65)

Café del Ángel

Guarding the small, heavenly square behind the Iglesia del Santo Ángel Custodio, minimalist Fumero's mega-popular outdoor tables are excellent perches for egg-based breakfasts and intimate dissections of Havana street life. (p64)

LISTINGS

Best Places for...

See p40 for map of locations

$ Budget $$ Midrange $$$ Top End

Eating

Breakfast & Brunch Spots

Café del Ángel $$$
22 C2
In the stunning Plazuela de Santo Ángel, this is the perfect place for breakfast and a coffee in the morning sunshine on the outdoor patio. *8am-10pm*

El Café $$
 23 C4
The city's most well-known brunch casual spot with a veggie-friendly menu and fresh bread, pancakes, sandwiches, and all kinds of juices and smoothies. *8am-5pm*

Star Café $$
24 D2
Playfully inspired by the Starbucks brand, this cafe has a wide variety of breakfast and brunch dishes, including French toast, pancakes, croissants, crepes and coffee. *7am-2am*

Loft Bahia $$$
 25 F6
A luxury brunch option every Sunday with DJs on the rooftop and plenty of cocktails and sea breeze, although the food and drinks are delicious at any time, any day of the week. *10am-4pm*

Esto No Es Un Café $$
 26 D3
Although its name states that it's not a cafe, it certainly does look, feel and taste like one. Delicious crepes and coffee. *8am-midnight*

Café El Escorial $
27 E5
A pleasant coffee shop on Plaza Vieja with an old-fashioned feel where they roast their own coffee and serve sweet treats. *9am-10pm*

Casual Dining

Doña Eutimia $$
 28 D2
Everyone's favorite place to go for hearty Cuban food that feels home cooked, located just off Plaza de la Catedral in an adorable side street. *noon-10pm*

Fonda al Pirata $$
 29 D3
Pirate-themed bar and restaurant next to Plaza de la Catedral with lunch options such as sandwiches, burgers and great drinks. Always busy and upbeat. *8am-midnight*

El Chanchullero $
 30 B5
A favorite for those on a budget; tuck into tasty and cheap dishes and quickly served cocktails on the small but packed rooftop. *1pm-midnight*

5 Esquinas Trattoria $$
 31 C2
Situated on the corner of the delightful Calle Espada with outdoor seating spilling onto the street. This restaurant does great oven pizzas and pasta dishes. *9:30am-10:30pm*

La Caribeña $
 32 C4
A simple place on Calle Obispo for you to pop into for no-fuss Cuban

food and good service. *9am-11pm*

Yucasabi $

 F3

An interesting concept that focuses on all-things yuca, Cuba's much-loved root vegetable, with dishes focusing on the country's culinary origins and regional cuisine. *10am-10pm*

La Esquina de Cuba $$

 D2

Large portions of classic Cuban dishes and well-prepared cocktails to be enjoyed on the small balcony. *11am-10pm*

Lo de Monik $$

 B2

Eschewing colonial splendor for a French bistro feel, Lo de Monik has a bright-white interior and arguably the city's friendliest staff. Search the blackboard menu for brunch or tapas ideas. *noon-11pm*

Kilómetro Zero $$

 B5

Touristy but touristy for a reason, this place always has great vibes and great food to match. The cocktails are as vibrant and colorful as the decor. *8am-2am*

Venami $

 B5

You could easily accidentally walk past this place, but this understated little restaurant does exceptional, authentic Italian food and is a favorite of those who know Havana well. *11:30am-11:30pm*

Paco's Mar $$

 E8

A casual, nautical-themed bar and restaurant by the waterfront that specializes in seafood and international cocktails. The Aperol spritzes are fantastic. *11:30am-midnight*

Habana 61 $$

 C2

Features Cuban classics with a fresh twist. The lobster is among its most popular dishes, but the traditional *ropa vieja* is just as delicious. The small restaurant can fill up quickly, so book ahead. *noon-midnight*

Fine Dining

5 Sentidos $$$

 C3

One of Havana's most high-end restaurants that really pushes the boat out when it comes to experimental fusion dishes and presentations. *noon-4pm, 6-11pm*

Al Carbón $$$

 B2

Owned by Fidel Castro's former chef, this restaurant, always packed and with frequent live music, has an open kitchen preparing succulent meats and vegetables roasted on the barbecue. *noon-midnight*

Antojos $$$

 C2

Always packed with Havana's most well-known and wealthy locals, this place has a great buzz, great service, and top-notch Cuban food and drinks. *11am-midnight*

Café Bohemia $$$

 E5

Top-end Italian cuisine with live music and a fantastic outdoor seating area in the middle of Plaza Vieja. Thin-crust pizzas, gelato and Italian-inspired cocktails. *7am-11pm*

La Vitrola $$$

 E5

A famous late-night spot in Old Havana with a musical theme and live music. It gets packed during weekends. *8:30am-2am*

Mythos $$$

 D3

Exceptional Greek cuisine, including fried feta cheese, souvlaki, and creative signature cocktails named after Greek gods and goddesses. The white and blue interiors are a nod to Greek design. *8am-11pm*

Paladar Los Mercaderes $$

 E4

An iconic paladar on Calle Mercaderes that serves fine dining with a decadent feel. Try to grab a seat on their balcony to watch the buzz below. *noon-midnight*

ChaChaChá $$$

47 B2

An elegant two-floor venue serving a mix of Cuban and international dishes such as risottos, pastas and sharing boards. *noon-midnight*

Buena Vista Curry Club $$$

 D2

If you're missing spicy food and are a bit bored of the typical Cuban fare, this authentic Indian restaurant is the place for you, as it does great curries with all the typical Indian side dishes. It's also a great option for vegetarians. *noon-midnight, closed Mon & Tue*

Jibaro $$

 E7

A small but inviting establishment known for its changing international menus, with Vietnamese food one week and Mexican, Turkish or Argentinian cuisine the next. *noon-11pm*

Drinking

Hemingway Haunts

El Floridita

 B4

The most famous (and touristy) bar in all of Cuba, thanks to Ernest Hemingway. This place was a former favorite of his, so pass by for a quick daiquiri, which was invented here. Take a photo with the statue of the writer leaning at the bar. *noon-1am*

Bodeguita del Medio

 D2

Another Hemingway haunt where he allegedly went to drink his mojitos (although this is contested). Very touristy but fun nonetheless. The walls are filled with the doodles and scribbles of past visitors. *10:30am-10:30pm*

Casual Bars

El Dandy

 B5

On lively Plaza del Cristo, this is a laid-back, boho café that turned into a super cool cocktail bar after dark. Choose from a blackboard of tacos, pastas and other small plates. *8am-midnight*

Bar Melodrama

 B4

Low-lit and low-key cocktail bar often frequented by the city's edgiest artists and bohemians, known as 'frikis.' Expect live acoustic and alternative music. *5pm-1am*

Máximo

 C1

Facing the seafront, this small open-air bar is always busy and has thumping music and delicious drinks. The *micheladas* are the perfect choice for a casual night out. *noon-1am*

Azúcar Lounge

 E5

From a 2nd-floor balcony high above Plaza Vieja, this drinking hole has loungey seating and good cocktails. *noon-midnight*

High-End Bars

Yarini

56 D8

Habana Vieja's most exclusive multi-level bar, where all the 'it' Cubans go. It turns from a restaurant to a cool club on the weekends with epic nighttime views. *4pm-midnight Mon-Fri, noon-2am Sat & Sun*

El del Frente

 D3

One of the most popular places in Old Havana; the piña coladas and gin and tonics are famous. Food highlights include *garbanzos fritos* (chickpea stew), octopus carpaccio, and crab tacos. *noon-midnight*

Ley Seca

 C4

Prohibition-style speak-easy-themed venue and one of the few very late-night places in Habana Vieja. Lots of dancing and shots. *11:30pm-4am*

Sibarita

 B4

Super centric rooftop bar on O'Reilly, close to Parque Central, with tiki-inspired cocktails, food with a tropical twist, and live DJs. *noon-midnight*

Fajoma

 C4

The place for cigar-lovers, as it has its own cigar lounge, great variety of rums and creative signature cocktails. *midnight-2am*

Habana 5 Restaurant

 C1

Climb the many flights of stairs to this rooftop venue with stunning views of the sea and the city, and fine dining cuisine and cocktails. *9am-2am*

Shopping

Clothing

Color Café

 C2

A cafe, workshop and clothing store selling beautifully tailored and designed pieces in interesting, eclectic fabrics. *8:30am-7pm*

Clandestina

 C5

Cuba's first independent fashion brand is famous for slogan tees, tote bags and cool caps made from recycled materials. They are responsible for the best runway shows and after-parties on the island. *10am-8pm*

Calore

64 C3

A luxurious clothing emporium featuring dozens of diverse Cuban fashion brands selling everything from luxury bikinis to ballgowns. Get handed a glass of wine and browse the beautifully curated collections. *11am-9pm*

Centro de las Raíces

65 B4

A pioneering store and salon with clothing, hair products, accessories, and other knick-knacks focused on Afro-Cuban identity and empowerment. *10am-6pm, closed Mon*

Cris-Cris

 C5

Eccentric high-fashion boutique on Plaza del Cristo specializing in barely-there underwear and swimwear. *hours vary*

Casa Fumero

 C2

Located in the beautiful Plazuela de Santo Ángel, this is one of Havana's most luxurious shops, with fashion from designer Jacqueline

Fumero, accessories, glassware, homeware, and beauty products. *10am-6pm, closed Mon*

Dador

68 D5

Another pioneering female-owned fashion brand that sells under-stated but very well-made garments for men and women in fabrics that are perfect for Cuba's humid climate. *11am-6pm*

Souvenirs

Matty Habana

69 D3

There is something for everyone in this bazaar featuring various Cuban brands, with clothing, toys, homeware, art and much more. *10am-5pm Mon-Sat, to 3pm Sun*

Real Fábrica de Tabacos Partagás

70 B4

A prestigious shop affiliated with Havana's main cigar factory. It sells some of Havana's best smokes and expert cigar aficionados are on hand to enlighten you. *9am-5pm*

Piscolabis Bazar & Café

 D3

This small but beautifully curated shop is run by a group of Cuban artists of various disciplines and features a wide range of decorative items, accessories and clothing. *10am-6pm*

La Feria de Publicaciones y Curiosidades

72 F3

Vintage flea market close to Plaza de Armas selling all manner of fascinating antiquities, including books, costume jewellery, memorabilia, and other gadgets and trinkets. The sellers are very knowledgeable and chatty. *9am-5pm*

Puchito's Shop

73 E6

The home and store of a passionate local record collector. This tucked-away space is tightly packed with Cuban vinyl everywhere you look, as well as other old objects. *10am-6pm*

Feria de Obispo

74 C4

Bustling market with typical tourist knick-knacks such as dominoes, wooden trinkets and crochet dresses. *10am-6pm*

L'Antigua Habana

75 F5

Down by the bay, this vintage outdoor market is mostly filled with books and magazines. *9:30am-5pm, closed Sun*

Casa Obbatalá

76 C6

This specialist religious shop sells all manner of Santería offerings and cult objects, almost exclusively to locals but it is fascinating to visit nonetheless. *8:30am-5pm Mon-Sat, 10am-1pm Sun*

Abanicos Habana

77 E4

A state-run shop selling *habaneros*' all-time favorite accessory: the hand fan. They are all hand-painted with flowers and swirls, and can even be personalized. These items are essential in the Cuban heat. *10am-5pm*

Art

Almacenes San José

78 E8

This large indoor artisan market is housed in former warehouses on the waterfront. Souvenirs are downstairs while Cuban art is upstairs. Most of the work tends to be very tourist-oriented (paintings of classic cars and sexy Cuban women), but there are always some gems to be found. *10am-6pm, closed Mon*

El Floridita (p66)
DAMIRA/SHUTTERSTOCK

Taller de Serigrafía René Portocarrero

79 E5

A state-run screenprinting workshop where you can browse contemporary designs and vintage Cuban posters. *9am-4pm*

Galería Máxima

80 B3

Around the corner from Bellas Artes, this space is an inventory of the best Cuban contemporary art for diverse tastes, curated by art collector Yaiset Ramírez. *10am-6pm*

La Marca

81 C7

Should you want a memento of your time in Cuba, try La Marca, which was the first licensed tattoo shop on the island. The parlor is run by young Cuban artists who maintain an international level of hygiene. *11am-7pm, closed Sun*

Factoría Diseño

82 F5

Contemporary art gallery in an industrial setting tucked down a side street close to the port with a mixture of visual art, design and artisanry for sale. *10am-5pm Mon-Sat*

See p88
for eating,
drinking and
shopping
listings

Explore
Centro Habana

Centro Habana's crowded residential grid offers an uncensored look at Cuba without the fancy wrapping paper. On its potholed but perennially action-packed streets, local kids fly down their barrio on *chivichanas* (wooden skateboards), elderly men engage in marathon games of dominoes, and women gossip with each other from across balconies. This is a particularly Afro-Cuban part of the city, where drums beat out addictive rumba rhythms from within homes, and you'll often see people dressed in all white sporting colorful beaded necklaces, a sign of their initiation into Santería. Hints of Centro's illustrious previous life can be seen at every turn, from the old Chinese quarter to Calle Galiano's faded grandeur.

Getting Around

Bici-taxi

As in Habana Vieja, there are hundreds of rickshaws posted around Centro Habana, raring to go. This is a great way of getting around Centro or to cross into Old Havana.

Public Transport

The best spot for transport is Centro's Parque Curita, where many public transport routes begin and end. Classic cars, moto-taxis, bici-taxis, minivans and shared taxis are all lined up on the park's northern side.

Walking

The best way to explore the winding streets of Centro Habana is on foot, where you can pick up on the idiosyncracies of local life in this downtrodden part of town.

THE BEST

ARCHITECTURAL GEM
Capitolio Nacional (p74)

ICONIC RESTAURANT
La Guarida (p78)

ROMANTIC PROMENADE
El Malecón (p80)

LOCAL LIFE
Street Life Tour (p82)

HISTORIC NEIGHBORHOOD
Barrio Chino (p81)

El Paseo del Prado (p77)
LENSFIELD/SHUTTERSTOCK

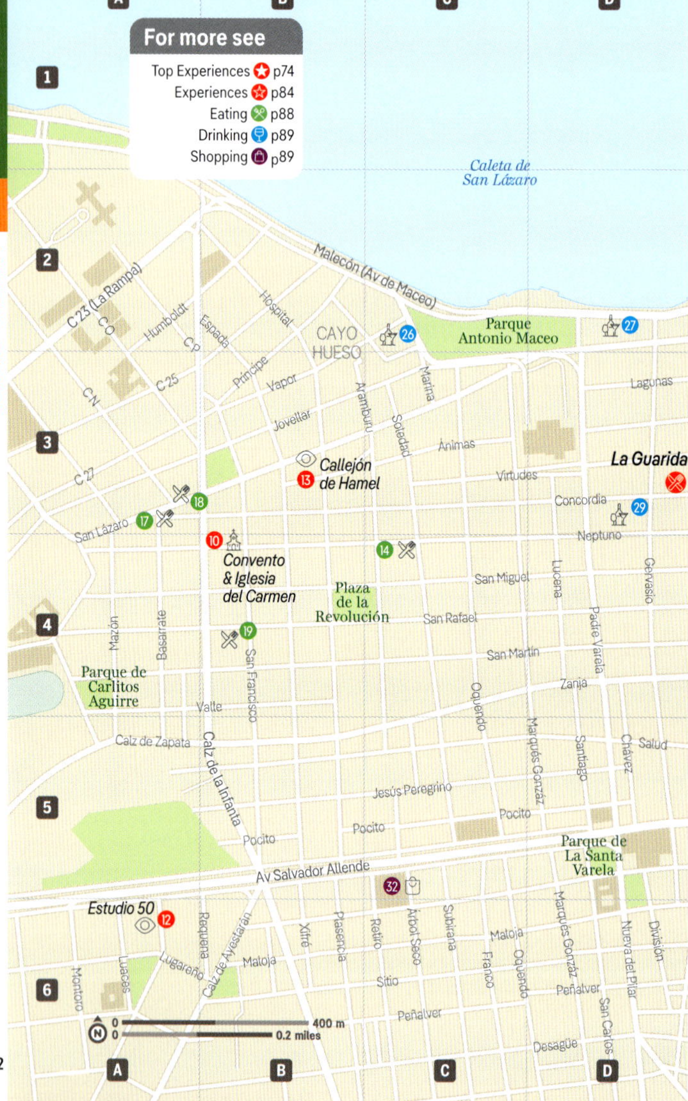
For more see
Top Experiences p74
Experiences p84
Eating p88
Drinking p89
Shopping p89
Caleta de San Lázaro
Malecón (Av de Maceo)
Parque Antonio Maceo
CAYO HUESO
C23 (La Rampa)
Humboldt
Espada
Hospital
Príncipe
Vapor
Jovellar
Aramburu
Soledad
Marina
Lagunas
Ánimas
Virtudes
La Guarida
Concordia
Neptuno
Callejón de Hamel
San Lázaro
Convento & Iglesia del Carmen
Plaza de la Revolución
San Miguel
San Rafael
San Martín
Zanja
Lucena
Padre Varela
Gervasio
Mazón
Basarrate
San Francisco
Parque de Carlitos Aguirre
Valle
Calz de Zapata
Calz de la Infanta
Oquendo
Marqués González
Santiago
Chávez
Salud
Jesús Peregrino
Pocito
Parque de La Santa Varela
Av Salvador Allende
Estudio 50
Requena
Calz de Ayestarán
Lugareño
Luaces
Montoro
Maloja
Xifré
Plasencia
Retiro
Árbol Seco
Subirana
Franco
Sitio
Peñalver
Desagüe
Nueva del Pilar
División
San Carlos
400 m
0.2 miles

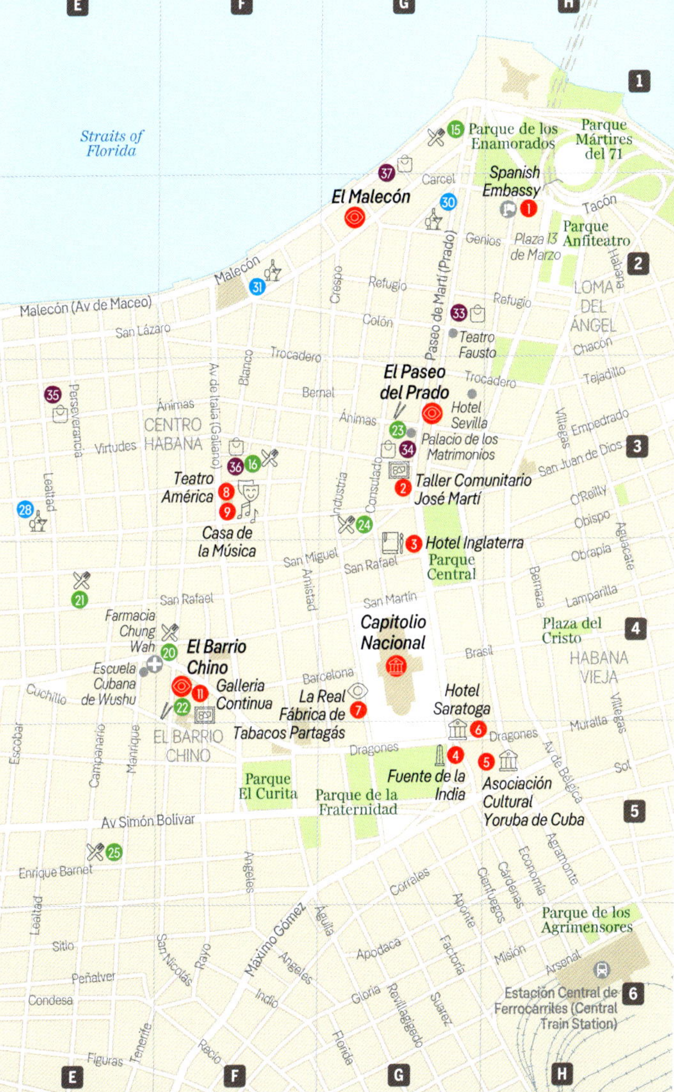

E
F
G
H
1
2
3
4
5
6
Straits of Florida
Parque de los Enamorados
Parque Mártires del 71
Spanish Embassy
El Malecón
Carcel
Tacón
Parque Anfiteatro
Genios
Plaza 13 de Marzo
Habana
Malecón
Malecón (Av de Maceo)
Crespo
Refugio
Paseo de Martí (Prado)
LOMA DEL ÁNGEL
Colón
Teatro Fausto
Chacón
San Lázaro
Trocadero
Blanco
Av de Italia (Galiano)
El Paseo del Prado
Tejadillo
Bernal
Perseverancia
Ánimas
Hotel Sevilla
Empedrado
CENTRO HABANA
Virtudes
Palacio de los Matrimonios
Villegas
San Juan de Dios
Lealtad
Teatro América
Industria
Consulado
Taller Comunitario José Martí
O'Reilly
Obispo
Casa de la Música
Hotel Inglaterra
Aguacate
San Miguel
San Rafael
Parque Central
Obrapía
Amistad
Bernaza
Lamparilla
San Rafael
San Martín
Farmacia Chung Wah
Capitolio Nacional
Plaza del Cristo
El Barrio Chino
Brasil
HABANA VIEJA
Escuela Cubana de Wushu
Barcelona
Hotel Saratoga
Cuchillo
Galleria Continua
La Real Fábrica de Tabacos Partagás
Villegas
Muralla
Escobar
Campanario
Manrique
EL BARRIO CHINO
Dragones
Dragones
Av de Bélgica
Sol
Parque El Curita
Fuente de la India
Asociación Cultural Yoruba de Cuba
Parque de la Fraternidad
Av Simón Bolívar
Enrique Barnet
Ángeles
Corrales
Economía
Agramonte
Aponte
Cienfuegos
Cárdenas
Lealtad
Máximo Gómez
Águila
Parque de los Agrimensores
Sitio
San Nicolás
Rayo
Apodaca
Factoría
Misión
Arsenal
Ángeles
Peñalver
Condesa
Indio
Gloria
Revillagigedo
Suárez
Estación Central de Ferrocarriles (Central Train Station)
Tenerife
Figuras
Recio
Florida
EXPLORE
CENTRO HABANA

★ TOP EXPERIENCE

Capitolio Nacional

The incomparable Capitolio Nacional is Havana's most ambitious and grandiose building, constructed after the post-WWI boom ('Dance of the Millions') gifted the Cuban government a seemingly bottomless vault of sugar money. This building is Havana's stunning gilded guardian and an iconic part of the city's skyline.

MAP P72 **G4**

QUICK BREAK
There are many spots to eat and drink a short walk from El Capitolio. Your closest option for a coffee and a bite is **Café El Capitolio** next door to the bookshop.

Scan this QR code for more detailed info on the history of the capitol.

Construction & Refurbishment

Although it's widely believed that El Capitolio was modeled on the Capitol building in Washington DC, with the Cuban version being ever so slightly taller, it actually took inspiration from the Panthéon in Paris. The building was initiated by Cuba's US-backed dictator Gerardo Machado in 1926, and it took 5000 workers only three years to construct this masterpiece, at a cost of US$17 million. Formerly the Capitolio was the seat of the Cuban Congress, then from 1959 to 2013 it housed the Cuban Academy of Sciences and the National Library of Science and Technology. From 2010, the building underwent an eight-year refurbishment, reopening just in time for Havana's 500th anniversary as Cuba's National Assembly in 2019.

The Entrance

The entryway is accessed by a sweeping 55-step staircase guarded by two giant statues carved by Italian sculptor Angelo Zanelli: *El Trabajo* (male) and *La Virtud Tutelar* (female). The three grand entrance doors with roaring lion knockers and Greek decorative designs narrate the story of Cuba in bronze: the left-hand side depicts the arrival of Christopher Columbus, the middle door the

LJUPCO SMOKOVSKI/SHUTTERSTOCK

nation's independence from Spain, and on the right the Cuban Revolution.

Salón de los Pasos Perdidos

These doors open into the Salón de los Pasos Perdidos (Room of the Lost Steps), so named because of its unusual acoustics. At its center point, directly under the cupola, stands a magnificent statue of La República, an enormous bronze woman standing 17.6m tall and symbolizing the mythic Guardian of Virtue and Work. The muse that inspired the work was Cuban Creole model Lily Valty. The 30-tonne statue is cast in bronze and covered in gold leaf and is the third-largest indoor statue in the world. It was carved by Zanelli in Rome and shipped to Cuba in three pieces.

PLANNING TIP

Ask if it's possible to see La Tumba del Mambí Desconocido (the Crypt of the Unknown Mambí), a hidden spot in El Capitolio that honors the *mambises*, independence fighters in the 19th century.

HOW TO BOOK
Admission is by guided tour only and tickets can be bought at the bookshop across the road with a debit or credit card (cash is not accepted). Hour-long guided tours in English and Spanish leave at 10am, 11am, 2pm and 3pm from Tuesday to Saturday; Sunday and Monday are closed. Tickets cost $20 and entrance is free for under 12s. Don't forget to bring your passport for ID.

A Hidden Gem

In the floor of the entrance hall is a giant 25-carat replica **diamond** encased in glass and in the center of a bronze star, marking 'Kilómetro Cero,' the starting point of Cuba's highway system. The original was mysteriously stolen in 1946, despite being under high-security surveillance. More curious still, the jewel was then handed back anonymously on the office table of the then-president Grau San Martín a year later. The real diamond is currently said to be protected in the National Bank of Cuba.

Other Rooms

Guided tours will take you around several of the 19 main areas, where you will be able to peep into sumptuous governmental offices furnished in exuberant French rococo and Empire styles. Wrought iron, dark mahogany wood, Italian marble, and French lamps and chandeliers (some weighing a ton) are all prominent parts of the interior design. The ornamentation's attention to detail is astounding, from the fixtures to wallpaper, and floor patterns, which all incorporate Cuban emblems such as palm trees, sugarcane and laurel leaves. The **Gran Biblioteca José Martí** is also a standout room, a grand library now without any books, but with plenty of decorative wallpaper, a marble figurehead of Martí and stunning globe lights. Two legislative chambers lie at either end of the building: the chamber of representatives and the chamber of deputies (the Senate). Also visable are two inner courtyards that help control temperatures in the building and add welcome splashes of green. In the center of one of the gardens is a statue of Lucifer, the leader of the angels who disobeyed God and were kicked out of Heaven. The work is a communist metaphor for independence and rebellion.

★ TOP EXPERIENCE

El Paseo del Prado

Paseo de Martí – or El Prado as locals call it – is a tree-lined boulevard that separates Old from Central Havana. Stretching from the Malecón sea promenade all the way to Capitolio Nacional, it contains a broad central walkway.

MAP P72 **G3**

Prado's Past

The street's layout took shape in the 1770s when it became the first proper thoroughfare to penetrate outside Havana's old city walls. In the 1920s, French landscape architect Jean-Claude Forestier added major embellishments, including four large bronze lions that were posted at either end.

Architectural Marvels

No matter which way you look, the architecture on both sides of the boulevard is spectacular if crumbling in places. Buildings to look out for include the neo-Renaissance **Palacio de los Matrimonios**, **Hotel Sevilla**, the streamlined art deco **Teatro Fausto** and the neoclassical **Escuela Nacional de Ballet** (p63), the world's largest ballet school and one of its most prestigious.

Local Walkway Turned into a Runway

El Prado is where many youths like to congregate, so get ready to practice your sidestepping skills with soccer-playing kids, street dancers and skateboarders. You'll also find older residents playing games of chess on the stone benches, dog walkers and partners on a romantic stroll. In 2016, during Cuba's short-lived economic boom due to the easing of US sanctions, El Prado was the chosen location for a Chanel fashion show, a momentous occasion for the city that garnered worldwide attention.

PLANNING TIP

Head to Prado on the weekend to see this walkway lined with Cuban artists producing, displaying and selling their work. Sunday is the best day.

★ TOP EXPERIENCE

La Guarida

The entrance to the city's most legendary private restaurant greets you like a scene out of a 1940s film noir. A decapitated statue lies at the bottom of a grand but dilapidated staircase that leads past lines of drying clothes to a wooden door, beyond which lie multiple culinary surprises.

MAP P72 **D3**

PLANNING TIP
La Guarida hosts rooftop jazz nights every Friday at 8:30pm with the crème de la crème of Cuban musicians performing. Reservations must be made in advance.

Scan this QR code for more information and to book a table.

Cinematic Dining Experience

La Guarida first came onto Havana's burgeoning culture scene in the 1990s, when it was used as a location for the Oscar-nominated film *Fresa y Chocolate*, a classic of Cuban cinema which touches on LGBTIQ+ community and post-Soviet hardship on the island. In 1996 La Guarida officially opened as a paladar, Cuba's first privately owned restaurants that were typically housed in people's homes. Since then, it has seen a cast of star-studded international guests pass through its doors, including Madonna, Jack Nicholson and Leonardo DiCaprio. La Guarida was even the location for a Rihanna photoshoot for *Vanity Fair* in 2015.

Havana's Hottest Hideout

This restaurant's name, meaning 'The Hideout,' is certainly fitting, as making your way up the maze of staircases and dusty doorways can feel thrilling and slightly disorientating. There is perhaps no place in the city that conveys the mood of Havana like this 1913 building, previously called 'La Mansión Camaguey,' turned luxury dining establishment. As is common in Cuba, you have to pass through locals' homes with their pets prowling around and washing hung up to dry to reach the hidden gem within.

JON ARNOLD IMAGES LTD/ALAMY

Step inside...

It's hard to believe that La Guarida started with just 12 seats; now it is a decadent labyrinth inside, with long, narrow corridors leading to various dining zones. The indoor salons are stylishly cluttered with black-and-white photographs and striking art on the mustard-colored walls, memorabilia taking up every surface, and crystal chandeliers dangling. Alfresco areas are more minimalist, with pretty string lights and fresh white tablecloths. Wind up the iron spiral staircase to a swanky rooftop bar that looks out over ramshackle Centro Habana. In terms of the food, the restaurant serves sophisticated takes on classics such as *ropa vieja* and less typically Cuban ones like lamb tikka masala.

DRINK BREAK

Across the road is Michifú (p89), a jazzy ground-level bar that's a good place to go for a more low-key drink before or after La Guarida.

★ TOP EXPERIENCE

El Malecón

Sometimes dubbed 'the world's longest sofa,' the iconic Malecón is a sweeping 7km-long sea drive that stretches from the cusp of Habana Vieja to the fringes of Miramar, incorporating some of the city's most evocative monuments and buildings, and is a sacredly special place for all locals.

MAP P72 **G2**

PLANNING TIP
To soak in sea views, grab a cocktail in the art-filled rooftop of Malecón 663 (p89) or the seriously swanky El Bleco (p89). Another less boozy pastime is to run the length of the Malecón at sunset or sunrise.

Setting the Scene

There may be no place in Havana that conjures up more nostalgia, romance and bittersweetness than El Malecón. This seawall has been the location of many a Cuban film scene, historic protests, first kisses and drunken gatherings. *Habaneros* of all types congregate here to gossip, party, meditate and masquerade, using the corroded seawall like it's an alfresco extension of their living rooms.

Havana Sunsets

The atmosphere intensifies at sunset, when the sky turns a streaky orange, giving the breathtaking Havana cityscape a distinctly romantic and hazy glow. The Malecón is transformed when a cold front blows in and massive waves crash over the sea wall. The road is often closed to cars at these times, meaning you can walk along the middle of the street and get a thorough soaking.

What to See along the Malecón

Neglect and the destructive effects of the ocean have left many of the waterfront thoroughfare's buildings facing serious decrepitude. However, there are several sites still in good shape along the Malecón, such as Vedado's Hotel Nacional and the US Embassy, bars and boutique hotels in Centro, and views of nearby fortresses in Habana Vieja.

★ TOP EXPERIENCE

El Barrio Chino

With its main entrance guarded by a giant pagoda and its street signs rendered in Roman and Chinese script, El Barrio Chino presents an authentic veneer. However, its Chinese residents left the island soon after socialist Fidel came to power. Regardless, it's worth investigating to hunt for remnants of Cuba's Asiatic past.

MAP P72 **F4**

The Chinese in Cuba

The first Chinese arrived in Havana as contract laborers in the late 1840s, and by the 1920s the city's Chinatown had become the biggest Asian neighborhood in Latin America. Walk around the neighborhood and look out for plaques written in Chinese and Spanish with the word 'sociedad,' a hint at past Chinese societies, a few of which are still active. You may also notice some residents with Asian features.

Calle Zanja

On the barrio's main thoroughfare, you will find the odd Chinese-influenced shop selling bonsai plants and the **Farmacia Chung Wah**, offering traditional Chinese medicinal lotions and potions and imported Asian products.

Calle Cuchillo

Calle Cuchillo is a lot more what you'd expect from a typical Chinatown, a narrow alleyway with Chinese decorations, although it's more of a veneer than anything else. However, one restaurant stands out among the rest: **Tien-Tan** (p88), an authentic restaurant owned by Roberto Vargas Li, a Cuban of Chinese descent who is a pillar of the Barrio Chino community. Every Saturday and Sunday at 9pm the restaurant has live Cuban music and traditional Chinese lion dance performances.

PLANNING TIP

Tien-Tan owner Roberto also owns **Escuela Cubana de Wushu**, an open-air space that holds morning martial arts classes such as tai chi. Message Roberto to liaise. (Whatsapp: +53 52977257)

Scan this QR code to find out about the efforts to revive and preserve El Barrio Chino

Centro Habana Street Life

Life in Centro Habana goes on irrespective of tourism, inclement weather or the distractions of the internet age. During the day this ebullient but dilapidated neighborhood is a microcosm of Cuban life – it's the city's most densely populated district, with 135,000 people squeezed into a 3-sq-km grid.

START	END	LENGTH
Prado and Trocadero	Cayo Hueso	3.5km, 1½ hours

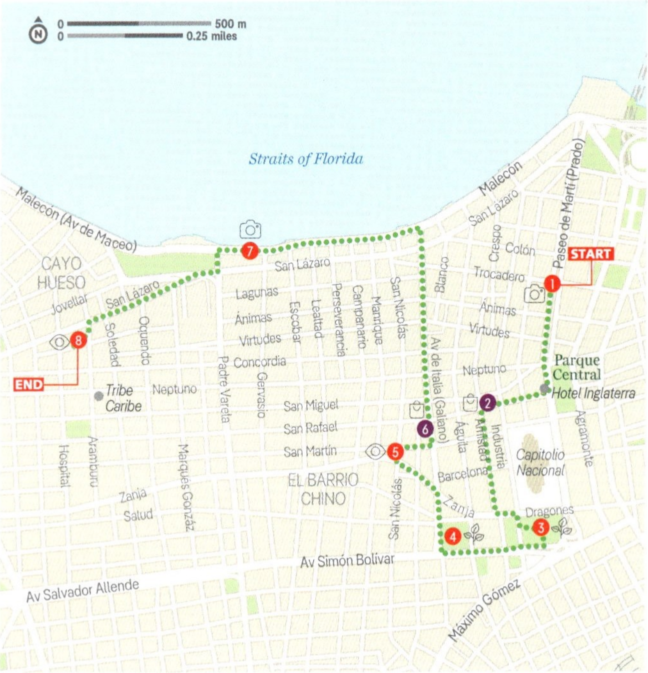

1 Leafy Walkway

Havana's finest walkway, **El Prado** (p77) is a key people-watching spot on this Centro Habana tour. Take in kids clumsily rollerblading, hordes of teens blaring reggaeton out on tinny speakers and elderly people playing rounds of chess.

2 Busiest Boulevard

The pedestrianized section of Calle San Rafael near Hotel Inglaterra (p84), known to *habaneros* as **El Bulevar**, is an unashamedly local affair, with super-cheap fast-food kiosks, *pan con lechón* (roast-pork sandwich) stalls, half-bare stores and 1950s shopping nostalgia. This is as Cuban as it comes.

3 In the Shadow of El Capitolio

Dozens of *almendrones* wait around the Capitolio in what has been dubbed Jurassic Park. The park's real name, **Parque de la Fraternidad**, is meant to signify brotherhood with the Americas, hence the busts of American leaders.

4 Lively Hub

The small **Parque Curita** is always buzzing with life, as it's Centro's most important transport nexus. Bici-taxis, regular taxis and public transport are all crammed into these narrow streets and it's a good way to take in the chaotic sights and sounds of everyday Havana life.

5 Welcome to Chinatown

El Barrio Chino (p81) is notable for its lack of Chinese residents. However, in the 1990s the Cuban government recognized the area's tourist potential and sought to rejuvenate its historical character. Look for signs of the city's almost-forgotten Chinese past.

6 Faded Grandeur

The street officially called Avenida de Italia is still referred to by *habaneros* as **Calle Galiano**. Serving as Centro Habana's main drag, it was once lined with plush department stores. These days, its demeanor is more downbeat, although the action is just as lively.

7 Iconic Ocean Odyssey

Glimpse the uncensored Cuba on Havana's 7km-long **Malecón** (p80) sea drive, where hundreds of *habaneros* come to stroll at sunset.

8 Afro-Cuban Hub

The cauldron full of old sticks is a *nganga* (Palo Monte altar) and the people dressed in white are *Iyabós* (Santería initiates). Welcome to **Cayo Hueso**, a subdistrict of Centro Habana with a strong Afro-Cuban heritage. The area is centered on Callejón de Hamel (p87), a paint-spattered alley rightly famous for its Sunday rumba drummers. Finish with a drink at a boutique hotel, coffee shop and rooftop bar, Tribe Caribe (p88).

EXPERIENCES

Visit Havana's Most Beautiful Embassy
EMBASSY BUILDING

MAP: 1 P72 H1

Now the **Spanish Embassy**, this beautiful wedding-cake-like building, Palacio Velasco, was constructed in art nouveau style in 1912. It's the only embassy in this part of town. Expect to see lines of paperwork-wielding Cubans on any day of the week as they hope to get their visa applications approved to move to Spain.

Browse Community Artwork
ART GALLERY

MAP: 2 P72 G3

Taller Comunitario José Martí is a workshop-gallery of an avant-garde artists' collective comprising around a dozen members. Enter via the radiant mural in El Prado to admire and/or buy probing, cutting-edge creations and chat to their makers.

Watch The World Go by at Havana's Oldest Hotel
HISTORIC HOTEL

MAP: 3 p72 G4

Hotel Inglaterra opened its doors in 1856 on the site of a popular bar called El Louvre (the hotel's alfresco bar still bears that name). Facing leafy Parque Central (p53), the building exhibits the neoclassical design features in vogue at the time, complemented by a lobby beautified with Moorish tiles. At a banquet here in 1879, José Martí made a speech advocating Cuban independence, and much later, US journalists covering the Spanish-American War stayed here.

Pass by a Fabulous Fountain
FOUNTAIN

MAP: 4 P72 G5

Spare a glance for the white Carrara-marble **Fuente de la India**, carved by Giuseppe Gaggini in 1837 for the Count of Villanueva and now situated on a traffic island in front of Hotel Saratoga. It portrays a regal indigenous woman adorned with a crown of eagle's feathers and seated on a throne surrounded by four gargoylesque dolphins.

Uncover Santería Secrets
MUSEUM

MAP: 5 P72 H5

To untangle the mysteries of the Santería religion, its saints and their powers, decamp to this museum-cultural center, **Asociación Cultural Yoruba de Cuba**. Aside from sculpted effigies of the various *orishas* (deities), the association hosts *tambores* (Santería drum ceremonies) on Friday at 6pm. Check the noticeboard at the door for details. Note that there's a church dress code for the *tambores* (no shorts or tank tops).

Glimpse the Facade of Hotel Saratoga
HISTORIC HOTEL

MAP: 6 P72 G5

Hotel Saratoga was one of Havana's most popular and luxurious hotels, where Beyoncé and Jay-Z famously chose to stay. Tragically, in 2022, a gas leak caused an explosion that practically blew the whole hotel apart and left dozens dead or injured. The hotel is now a shell of its former self (literally) and is slowly being reconstructed.

Tour a Top Cuban Cigar Factory
FACTORY

MAP: 7 P72 G4

One of Havana's oldest and most famous cigar businesses, **La Real Fábrica de Tabacos Partagás** was founded in 1845 by Spaniard Jaime Partagás. In 2013, the factory moved from its original location behind the Capitolio (p74) to its current digs just off Calle Padre Varela in Centro Habana. It's the only cigar factory in Havana offering reliable tours that take you around the rat-runs and inner workings of the factory floor, where you can see the highly skilled drying, rolling, cutting, selecting and packaging processes. Tickets must be bought beforehand in the lobby of any of the hotels on Parque Central.

See a Show at an Art Deco Theater
THEATER

MAP: 8 P72 F3

Housed in a classic art deco *rascacielo* (skyscraper), **Teatro América** seems to have changed little since its theatrical heyday in the 1930s and '40s. It hosts variety, comedy, dance, jazz and salsa; shows are normally held on Saturday at 8:30pm and on Sunday at 5pm. If you don't have time for a performance, you should definitely pass by to see the architecture.

CUBA'S GOLDEN ERA

Havana in the 1940 and '50s was glamorous and cosmopolitan, said to be one of the most developed cities in Latin America at the time, even outpacing some US and European cities. Dubbed the 'Paris of the Caribbean,' Havana had world-class entertainment, a booming financial and tourism sector, and highly developed infrastructure such as transport and electricity. It wasn't all glitz and glamor, though. The city, and indeed the country, suffered from severe social inequality and corruption from the Cuban government and notorious foreign mobsters. The Instagram account @iwashavana will give you a glimpse into pre-revolutionary life in the capital through vintage photography.

Dance at the House of Music

MUSIC VENUE

MAP: 9 P72 F3

One of three such establishments in the city, **Casa de la Música** is a legendary place where Cubans and tourists go for full-on caliente music and salsa dancing. All the big names play here, from Bamboleo to Los Van Van – and you'll pay peanuts to see them. Even if you don't want to be pulled up onto the dance floor, sit in a corner and watch the whirling dancing and flirting of the crowds.

Step into Centro's Convent

CHURCH

MAP: 10 P72 B4

This little-visited church, **Convento & Iglesia del Carmen**, features a bell tower that dominates the Centro Habana skyline and is topped by a huge statue of Nuestra Señora del Carmen, but the real prizes are inside: rich Seville-style tiles, a gilded altarpiece, ornate woodcarving and swirling frescoes. Surprisingly, the church was only constructed in 1923 to house a Carmelite order. The building is considered 'eclectic.'

Explore Contemporary Art in an Old Chinese Cinema

ART GALLERY

MAP: 11 P72 F4

Set in an old Chinese cinema in Barrio Chino, this cutting-edge contemporary gallery is a hidden treasure in Centro Habana. **Galleria Continua** has frequent exhibitions showcasing Cuban talent as well as some permanent pieces from international artists such as Anish Kapoor.

Witness a Warehouse Party

CULTURAL VENUE

MAP: 12 P72 A6

One of the most popular cultural spaces in Havana, **Estudio 50** is set in a former abandoned warehouse on the Centro/Vedado/Cerro divide, hosting regular exhibitions, events and live music nights.

THE RISE OF THE GRAFITEROS

Subtly nuanced works by Cuban artists are often loaded with hidden messages or *doble sentido* (double meaning) and can deliver a powerful political message while still being careful how they frame their ideas. Unauthorized graffiti is a relatively new phenomenon and one of the city's most daring and visible new *grafiteros* is Fabian, known for his tag 2+2=5? and his recurring character, 'supermalo,' a cartoonish minion masked by a balaclava, used to make comments about contemporary culture. Other *grafiteros* include Fichu, known for his hallmark sultry Afro-Cuban women full of attitude, and Mr Sad, who writes 'necesitas ser feliz' (you need to be happy) all over town.

Callejón de Hamel
ALVARFUENTE/SHUTTERSTOCK

Wander down an Afro-Cuban-Themed Alleyway

STREET ART

MAP: 13 P72 B3

There are at least four reasons that you should incorporate this community-driven back alley into any serious Havana outing: first, **Callejón de Hamel** is the unofficial HQ of Havana's Afro-Cuban community; second, it's replete with inspired street art, much of it executed with recycled materials (this is where your old bathtub gets a new life); third, it's an essential stop for anyone trying to understand Cuba's complex syncretic religions; and, fourth, the denizens put on hypnotic live rumba shows on Sundays.

LISTINGS

Best Places for...

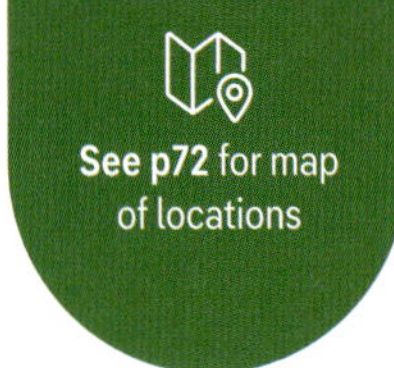

$ Budget $$ Midrange $$$ Top End

Eating

Cafes

Tribe Café $$

 C4

The cafe of boutique hotel Tribe Caribe. Hearty sandwiches, burgers, and light bites such as bruschetta. *8am-5pm*

Origen $$$

 G1

This hotel cafe does a top selection of luxurious cakes, pastries and chocolates. This is an indulgent experience with tranquil sea views. *10am-8pm*

Cafe Arcángel $

 F3

A homely cafe in the heart of Centro with good coffee and simple breakfasts comprising fresh fruit, eggs, toast and warm croissants. *8:15am-6pm, closes 1pm Sun*

Lunch

Locos por Cuba $

17 A3

An eccentric little cafe and restaurant filled with photographs with a cheap and simple yet tasty menu. Great for a light meal, a snack and a drink on its tiny balcony. *9am-11pm*

El Biky $$

 A3

Super-popular meet-the-locals brunch-lunch spot with quick-fire food served to a backdrop of retro photos. It has added a cool bar and Havana's best bakery next door. *8am-midnight*

San Rafael 1051 $$

 B4

Succulent hamburgers are this colorful fast-food joint's specialty as well as crispy chicken nuggets and sandwiches. *noon-midnight*

La Juliana $$

 F4

This small diner in Barrio Chino is a local favorite, best known for its pizzas and ice-cream shakes and generous portions of Cuban food. *10am-11pm*

Dinner

San Cristóbal $

 E4

Famous for being visited by Barack Obama in 2016, this restaurant has a museum-worthy interior crowded with memorabilia and budget-friendly food. *noon-midnight, closed Sun*

Restaurante Tien-Tan $$

22 F4

An authentic Chinese restaurant in El Barrio Chino serving over 100 dishes. Sit outside in action-packed Calle Cuchillo, a narrow pedestrianized alley. *11am-midnight*

Restaurante MiThai $$

23 G3

On the picturesque El Prado, this gourmet Thai restaurant serves the typical suspects: fragrant green curries, hot pots, som tam and more. They also sometimes put on live cooking shows *11:30am-midnight Tue-Sun*

Tonyzz Bar $

24 G3

A stone's throw from Hotel Inglaterra, this humble restaurant serves authentic Sri Lankan cuisine and good cocktails. The lentil curry is a must-try. *noon-2am*

Baracoando $$
 E5

For a unique experience, this vegan restaurant is a Havana version of trailblazing chef Aristides Smith's original place in Baracoa in the east of the country. Must book a day in advance *(Whatsapp +53 52589319). 6-9pm*

Drinking

El Bleco
 C2

El Bleco has established itself as one of Havana's best bars. On the open-roofed sea-view terrace, DJs curate ambient music while waitstaff serve drinks and much-talked-about pizza. *6pm-2am Mon-Sat, 1pm-2am Sun*

Malecón 663
 D2

A super-artsy boutique hotel with a coffee shop by day and a rooftop bar at night, close to the Malecón. *5-11pm*

Michifú
 E3

An effortlessly cool piano bar with pop-art lamps and color-accented sofas. Flop down amid the cushions and imbibe rum-laced cocktails as local musical prodigies practice their Tchaikovsky. *noon-1am Tue-Sat*

La Concordia
 D3

Yet another great rooftop bar with Cuban cocktails and bites to eat with views over Centro Habana. *1pm-1am*

Bestview Havana
 G2

Cigar sunsets, rum and wine tastings, and dance and music nights all take place on the rooftop of this bar with 360-degree city views. *5-11pm*

Blanco 9
 F2

Sequestered in a short, narrow street just off the Malecón, a super-small but inviting setting good for a quick beer or Cuba Libre. *hours vary*

Shopping

Plaza Carlos III
 C5

There's not much for tourists but it's interesting to see what a shopping mall looks like in communist Cuba. The place has taken a step up: formerly empty shelves are now at least half full of consumer goods. *9:30am-6pm*

Casa Guerlain
33 G2

This exclusive perfume parlor reopened on the same premises as the original 1917 shop and sells high-end perfume and cosmetics. *hours vary*

Plan H
 G3

If you're tired of sugary rum cocktails, Havana's first wine bar and shop is a refreshing respite with a delicatessen attached. *11:30am-midnight Tue-Sun*

Guermantes
 E3

A concept store and studio by Havana fashionista Monica Ge Bravo, which customizes clothing for a vintage, retro and highly feminine feel. *11am-6pm Tue-Sat*

Akares Shopitrapo
 F3

Cubans are experts in the art of reusing and upcycling clothing. There are many garage sales in the city but this thrift store is a far more curated and official version. *9am-5pm*

Capicúa
 G1

Cuban fashion brand whose designs center around eclectic, bright fabrics and garments that can be worn in multiple ways. *hours vary*

See p111
for eating, drinking and shopping listings

Explore Vedado

When Habana Vieja and Centro began to overcrowd and lose their glamor, Havana's upper class decided to move further afield to build new, elegant mansions with more space and greenery. And so Vedado was born. After independence from Spain, US intervention ushered in serious capital and development, and this district is an example of this heavy North American influence. Vedado is Havana's once notorious Mafia-run district. This was (and still is) the city's commercial hub, although now the nightlife is less tawdry and the hotels have become historical relics. Juxtaposed with modernist skyscrapers is a leafy, spread-out residential quarter, with endless rows of decorative detached houses.

Getting Around

Public Transport

Vedado is easily accessible from most other points in Havana, especially Parque Central in Habana Vieja and Parque Curita in Centro. The two main transport hubs are Calle 23, especially around its intersection with Calle L, and Línea.

Walking

A lot of Vedado is walkable, and with its grid system with numbers and letters, it's very easy to get your bearings.

Taxis

Taxis wait outside the main hotels, including the Hotel Nacional and Hotel Habana Libre.

THE BEST

HISTORIC HOTEL Hotel Nacional (p94)

ENCHANTING CEMETERY Necrópolis Cristóbal Colón (p100)

REVOLUTIONARY SQUARE Plaza de la Revolución (p102)

ART HUB Fábrica de Arte Cubano (p98)

ELECTRIFYING JAZZ Fangio Habana (p111)

Che Guevara mural, Plaza de La Revolución (p102)
ALEXANDRE F FAGUNDES/SHUTTERSTOCK

A
B
C
D
500 m
0.25 miles
Straits of Florida
For more see
Top Experiences p94
Experiences p106
Eating p111
Drinking p113
Shopping p113
Casa de las Américas
Malecón
Centro Fidel Castro Ruz
Acosta Danza
Boca de la Chorrera
Casa de la Amistad
Parque Lennon
Ruta Bikes
El Cimarrón
Fábrica de Arte Cubano
VEDADO
Río Almendares
Calz de Zapata
Av Obispo Fray Jacinto
Av Cristóbal Colón
Necrópolis Cristóbal Colón
Paseo
Linea
Calzada
Av 5
Av 3

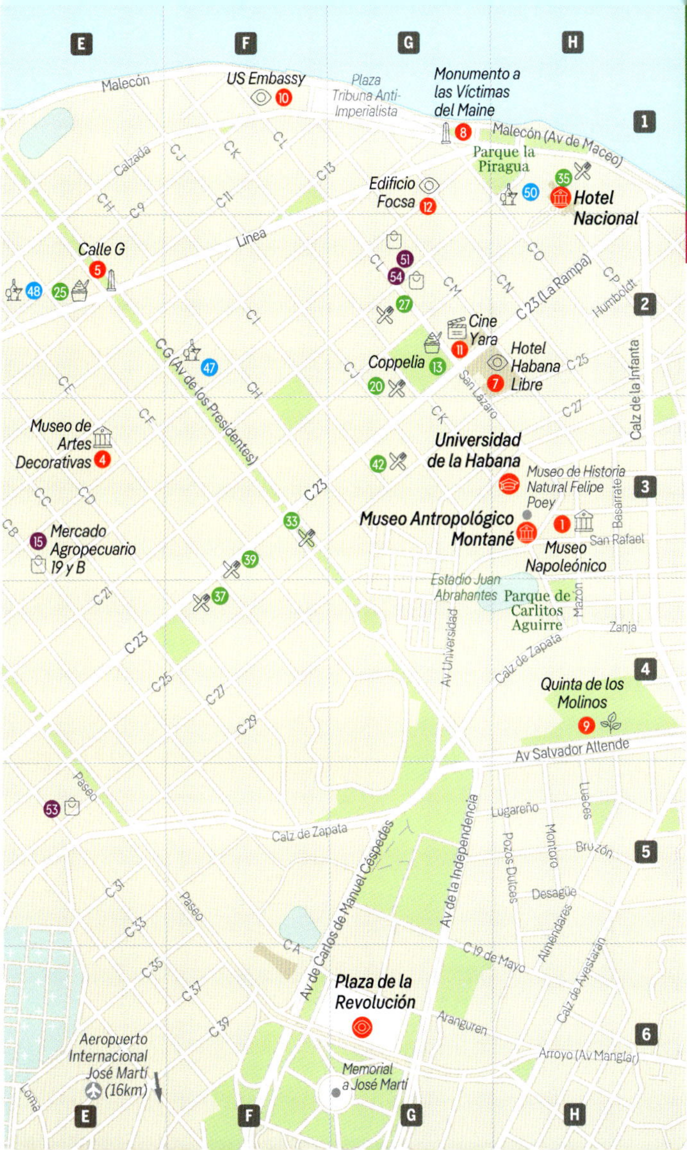

E F G H

1 2 3 4 5 6

US Embassy 10
Plaza Tribuna Anti-Imperialista
Monumento a las Víctimas del Maine 8
Malecón
Malecón (Av de Maceo)
Parque la Piragua
35
50
Hotel Nacional
Edificio Focsa 12
Calle G 5
48 25
51 54 27
Cine Yara 11
Hotel Habana Libre 7
Coppelia 13
20
47
Museo de Artes Decorativas 4
Universidad de la Habana
42
Museo de Historia Natural Felipe Poey
Museo Antropológico Montané
1 Museo Napoleónico
33
Mercado Agropecuario 19 y B 15
39
37
Estadio Juan Abrahantes
Parque de Carlitos Aguirre
Quinta de los Molinos 9
Av Salvador Allende
53
Plaza de la Revolución
Memorial a José Martí
Aeropuerto Internacional José Martí (16km)

Calzada, Linea, CH, C9, CJ, CK, CL, C11, C13, CO, CN, CM, CP, C23 (La Rampa), Humboldt, CI, CG (Av de los Presidentes), CE, CF, CJ, C25, San Lázaro, CK, C27, Calz de la Infanta, CC, CD, CB, C23, Basarrate, San Rafael, Mazón, Zanja, Av Universidad, Calz de Zapata, C21, C25, C27, C29, Paseo, Lugareño, Luaces, Calz de Zapata, Av de Carlos de Manuel Céspedes, Av de la Independencia, Pozos Dulces, Montoro, Bruzón, Desagüe, Almendares, C31, C33, C35, C37, C39, CA, C 19 de Mayo, Calz de Ayestarán, Aranguren, Arroyo (Av Manglar), Loma

★ TOP EXPERIENCE

Hotel Nacional

Far more than just a hotel, the Nacional, built in 1930 as a copy of the Breakers Hotel in Palm Beach, Florida, is a national monument and one of Havana's architectural emblems. Even if you're not staying here, reserve time for a drink in the famous terrace bar overlooking the Malecón.

MAP P92 **H1**

PLANNING TIP
The hotel has two swimming pools that offer day passes. Get to the reception early in the morning to pay by card, where a portion of the entrance fee includes food and drink served poolside.

Scan this QR code for more info on rooms and amenities.

The Sergeant's Coup

The hotel's notoriety was cemented in October 1933 when, following a sergeants' coup by Fulgencio Batista that toppled the regime of Gerardo Machado, 300 aggrieved army officers took refuge in the building hoping to curry favor with resident US ambassador Sumner Welles, who was staying there. Much to the officers' chagrin, Welles promptly left, allowing Batista's troops to open fire on the hotel, killing 14 officers and injuring seven. More were executed later, after they had surrendered.

The Havana Conference

In December 1946 the hotel gained infamy of a different kind when US mobsters Meyer Lansky and Lucky Luciano used it to host the largest ever get-together of the North American Mafia. The Cosa Nostra gathered here under the guise of a Frank Sinatra concert and convened a meeting that discussed Luciano's leadership, the growth of Mafia interests in Las Vegas and the potential of large-scale gambling in Cuba. In due course, Lansky went on to open up Havana's most luxurious casino in a refurbished wing of the hotel in 1955.

ION MES/SHUTTERSTOCK

Facilities

The flagship of the government-run Gran Caribe chain, the Hotel Nacional sports a hybrid of neo-classical, art deco and eclectic architectural styles. The richly tiled lobby is distinctly Moorish while the history-filled rooms are decorated with plaques advertising details of illustrious past occupants (Winston Churchill, Frank Sinatra and Errol Flynn among them).

The towering Havana landmark's sweeping manicured lawn is a famous place to grab a coffee or a cocktail, with panoramic views of the Florida Straights, live Cuban music and peacocks that roam the grounds. Ask at reception about free hotel tours, which include taking a look at the 'Hall of Fame' in the ground-floor Bay View Bar and a small museum dedicated to the 1962 Cuban Missile Crisis set up in an old military battery in the hotel grounds. Hotel Nacional also contains a cigar lounge rooftop bar, and top-class cabaret, the Parisien.

TAKE A BREAK

In the grounds of the hotel is its best restaurant, La Barraca (p112). Its outdoor terrace serves drinks and light bites, while the indoor restaurant offers delicious Cuban fare at decent prices.

★ TOP EXPERIENCE

Universidad de la Habana

Founded by Dominican monks in 1728 and secularized in 1842, Havana's university began life in Habana Vieja before moving to its present site in 1902. The existing neoclassical complex dates from the second quarter of the 20th century, and today some 30,000 students take courses here.

MAP P92 **H3**

PLANNING TIP

Aim to go Monday to Friday, preferably in the morning when the campus is more accessible. Expect the university to be closed on weekends and during semester breaks.

Scan this QR code for more information on the university.

A Grand Institution

Universidad de la Habana acts as a studious gatekeeper to the entrance of the Vedado neighborhood. With a sweeping entry stairway and slender Corinthian columns, it radiates a vaguely Aristotelian air. Perched in the main entrance is a bronze Alma Mater statue (pictured), constructed in 1919. The figure's face drew inspiration from a teen model named Feliciana Villalón, the daughter of a mathematics professor at the university. The campus has two museums. **Museo de Historia Natural Felipe Poey** is the oldest museum in Cuba, with many specimens of Cuban flora and fauna. **Museo Antropológico Montané** specializes in pre-Columbian artifacts, including a 10th-century Indigenous idol called the Ídolo del Tabaco.

Fidel Castro's Student Years

The university's most famous alumnus was undoubtedly Fidel Castro, who enrolled in a law degree in 1945. The campus was a breeding ground for the ideas that were forming in his mind at the time, which turned into vehement left-wing ideology. He quickly made himself a reputation for being confrontational and extroverted, engaging in anti-imperialist activism that tipped over into

DANIJEL LJUSIC/SHUTTERSTOCK

aggression on occasion. Fidel also honed his skills as a world-class orator through speeches that garnered press and public attention.

Revolutionary Hotbed

During this time, the university became notorious for *gangsterismo*, student activist groups whose violent and bloody run-ins made them more like rival gangs than fellow contemporaries with differing political ideologies. In the run-up to the Cuban Revolution, Havana University became a hotbed of revolutionary political thought and protests, most notably the failed assassination attempt of the then-leader Batista at the Presidential Palace in 1957. In the university's inner courtyard, filled with tropical greenery and areas for shade and tranquility, proudly stands a military tank that was captured by Castro's rebels in 1958, a homage to the contributions of students in the Revolutionary fight.

QUICK BREAK

A stone's throw from the university is the adorable little eatery Locos por Cuba (p88) on Calle San Lázaro. Sit on the tiny balcony overlooking this busy road and enjoy a coffee and/or a simple Cuban meal.

★ TOP EXPERIENCE

Fábrica de Arte Cubano

If only every city had a cultural venue as wide-ranging, inclusive and downright revolutionary as Havana's unique art factory. This gallery–live-music venue–inspirational meeting place for anyone who can afford the modest entry fee is where electrifying 'happenings' take place in a cavernous, Bauhaus-like interior.

MAP P92 **A5**

PLANNING TIP
On entering, you will be given a card, which bartenders will stamp each time you order a drink, and you pay your total bill when you leave the club. Lose the card and pay a hefty fine!

Scan this QR code to find out what's coming up at FAC.

Havana's Art Factory

Catapulting straight to the top of Havana's best nightlife spots when it opened in 2014, Vedado's unique art 'factory' was the brainchild of Cuban fusion musician X-Alfonso. First and foremost, FAC is an art gallery, with paintings, sculptures, graffiti, photography and installations on every wall and in every corner of this formerly abandoned factory. The space closes every three months (May, September and January) to make way for new exhibitions to be put up, making Fábrica a dynamic and ever-changing art experience. You'll likely come away from FAC saying, 'this is like nowhere I've been to before.' What makes the space so special is the diversity of not just its art but its public, where people of all ages, classes, and styles congregate to appreciate good culture, both Cuban and foreign.

Cultural Powerhouse

The concept of FAC is to house all of the arts under one roof. In Nave 3, you will find film screenings, fashion shows and dance performances. Nave 4 is the main stage, where famous artists perform. When particularly big artists come to play, FAC becomes heaving, so make sure to arrive

YAMIL LAGE/GETTY IMAGES

early to get a good spot. Nave 1 is an intimate space for newcomers and niche musical genres. Cool yet unpretentious, FAC is the kind of place where you can meet the performers as well as be part of the audience. Expect free tango lessons, classical cellists, Cuban rappers and dizzying rumba shows – all in the same night – so follow the sounds.

Best Nightlife Spot

FAC contains several bars dotted around the space serving incredibly strong drinks. It also has an exclusive VIP section with its own swanky bar, chill-out areas and a balcony that looks down onto the main stage. You can only get in if you're a 'somebody' in the creative world in Havana, however there is one loophole. Within VIP, there is a rooftop restaurant called **Tierra** (p112). Dine here and you'll get automatic access all night.

MEAL BREAK
Next door to FAC is El Cocinero (p112), at the top of a steep staircase inside an old factory tower. This is a great place for a fancy dinner before your big night out.

★ TOP EXPERIENCE

Necrópolis Cristóbal Colón

Havana's gigantic cemetery is the finest in the Americas and rightly renowned for its striking religious iconography and elaborate marble statues. A walk within these 57 hallowed hectares can be an educational and emotional stroll through the annals of Cuban history.

MAP P92 **D6**

PLANNING TIP
If you're short on time, stick to the main sights along Av Cristóbal Colón between Puerta de la Paz and the Capilla Central. Detailed maps are available from the ticket office for a small fee.

Scan this QR code for admission fees and opening hours.

The Vital Statistics

Completed in 1871 using the designs of Spanish architect Calixto de Loira, the cemetery is one of the world's largest, harboring more than 450 mausoleums and 800,000 graves. Around 1.5 million living souls visit it annually, and around 50 people are buried here per day. In fact, the cemetery is so crowded that some months after their loved ones are put to rest, families must return and move the deceased's remains into a small box to make space for new burials. It's laid out in a perfect grid, with the most important people interred along the main avenues. The cemetery is particularly beautiful and tranquil at sunset.

Puerta de la Paz

The main entrance, known as Puerta de la Paz (Peace Gate; pictured), is framed by a splendid Byzantine-Romanesque triple arch topped by a statue of Our Lady of Mercy, carved by Cuban sculptor José Villalta Saavedra in 1904. The neo-Romanesque Capilla Central (1886), in the exact center of the cemetery, is an unusual octagonal construction said to be modeled on Florence's Duomo. Rare is the day when you don't see at least one solemn funeral procession filing out of its hushed interior.

GARFOEMALA/SHUTTERSTOCK

La Milagrosa

Northeast of the Capilla Central is the graveyard's most celebrated tomb, that of Señora Amelia Goyri, better known as La Milagrosa (the miraculous one), who died while giving birth in 1901. When the bodies were exhumed some years later, Amelia's body was uncorrupted, and the baby, who had been buried at its mother's feet, was allegedly found in her arms. As a result, La Milagrosa became the focus of a huge spiritual cult in Cuba, and thousands of people come here annually with gifts, in the hope of fulfilling dreams or solving problems. In keeping with tradition, pilgrims knock with the iron ring on the vault and walk away backwards when they leave.

QUICK BREAK

On the edge of Vedado's main street, Calle 23, there are many eating options. On the corner of 23 and 18 is Panparapan (p112), where you can go for a cold Cristal beer and a pizza.

★ TOP EXPERIENCE

Plaza de la Revolución

Conceived by French urbanist Jean-Claude Forestier in the 1920s, the gigantic Plaza de la Revolución was part of Havana's 'new city,' which grew up between 1920 and 1959. Surrounded by gray, utilitarian buildings constructed in the late 1950s, the square today is the base of the Cuban government and a place where large-scale political rallies are held.

MAP P92 **G6**

PLANNING TIP
Classic car tours stop off here for tourists to take photos of the gray architecture behind bubble-gum pink Chevrolets and bright red Fords. If on foot, walk up beautiful Av Paseo to get to the square.

Scan for QR code for more history on Cuba's May Day Parade.

Always Toward Victory

In keeping with the original plan, the square was built on a small hill (Loma de los Catalanes) in the manner of Place de l'Étoile in Paris, with avenues fanning out in various directions toward Río Almendares, Vedado and Parque de la Fraternidad. The ugly concrete block on the northern side of the plaza is the Ministerio del Interior, well known for its huge mural of Che Guevara with the words *Hasta la victoria siempre* (Always Toward Victory) emblazoned underneath. The adjacent telecommunications building depicts Che's fellow revolutionary Camilo Cienfuegos, whose death in October 1959 is shrouded in conspiracy after a plane he was taking from Camaguey to Havana was said to have disappeared somewhere in the Caribbean Sea.

The Martí Memorial

The centerpiece of th Plaza de la Revolución is the **José Martí Memorial** (pictured), a monument entirely befitting the man celebrated as Cuba's national hero. It consists of a 138.5 m-tall star-shaped tower (which you can ascend by elevator), which was Havana's tallest structure until it was eclipsed by the K23 Tower in 2022. In front is a 17m marble statue of Martí crouched in a pensive pose. It mirrors the Lincoln Memorial in Washing-

PAULETTE PAIYEE/SHUTTERSTOCK

ton, DC, in both reverence and scale. At its base is a succinctly comprehensive museum that provides the definitive word on Martí's life and work, with photos and large panel displays.

May Day Parade

Every May 1, thousands of Cubans from all over the island congregate in La Plaza de La Revolución to celebrate International Workers' Day. Participants, typically state workers, students and union members, get up while it's still dark and start the long parade to the square while the sun comes up. People wave banners, flags and all kinds of revolutionary propaganda, and shout slogans, sing, dance and blow whistles, before the president makes a predictably socialist speech. While it doesn't draw the crowds it once did, it remains a major event in the capital.

QUICK BREAK
Before heading to the plaza, go for a brunch at gourmet restaurant Fangio Habana (p111) on Av Paseo, or go for a drink on the rooftop afterwards to cool down.

Vedado by Night

In Vedado's pre-revolution heyday, it was the party capital of the Americas. During prohibition, drinking-deprived Americans hopped over to indulge in the island's excesses in this district's casinos and cabarets. Although this era is a thing of the past, Vedado nightlife is still electric and edgy. So, enjoy this nocturnal stroll (or drunken stagger) around Vedado.

START	END	LENGTH
Submarino Amarillo	Club 23	2.5km; four-five hours

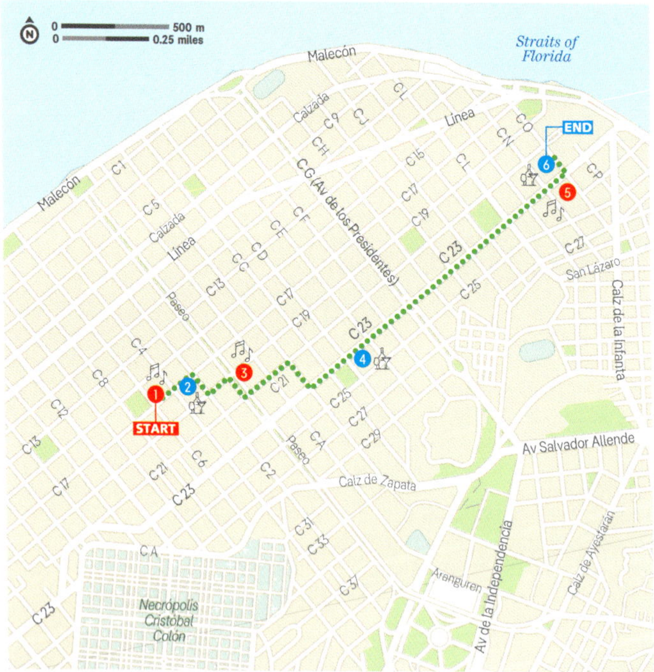

1 Beatles Tribute

No one knew much about Cuban *roqueros* (rock fans) until well into the 21st century. The groups that used to hang out clandestinely at the corner of Calles 23 and G have subsequently founded their own venue, **Submarino Amarillo**, a bar and live-music club with a bright-yellow interior that celebrates the Beatles but rocks to pretty much anything in 4/4 time.

2 Quirky Drinking Hole

Vedado flirts with bohemia in **Café Madrigal**, a dimly lit gay-friendly bar that might have materialized from the Latin Quarter in the days of James Joyce and Ernest Hemingway. Order a *tapita* (small tapa) and a cocktail, and retire to the atmospheric art nouveau terrace, where the buzz of nighttime conversation competes with the racket of vintage American cars rattling past below.

3 Rooftop Jazz

Fangio Habana (p111) is a restaurant at Claxon, a private boutique hotel in a handsome Vedado mansion on the beautiful Av Paseo, with a rooftop bar that's become the hottest place in the city to see live jazz. On most nights of the week, the terrace regularly pulsates to silky sounds as you witness world-class Cuban musicians while you nurse a glass of rum and a cigar.

4 Garish Discoteca

Between Calles D and E on Calle 23 is the infamous **King Bar**, whose name has a raunchy double meaning if you say it in Cuban Spanish. Formally a gay bar, it now welcomes clubbers of all sexual orientations, making it guaranteed to be packed almost every day of the week. Expect blasting reggaeton, Cuban music and nostalgic international chart-toppers until the early hours.

5 Underground Jazz Club

Further down Calle 23, also known as La Rampa, you'll find the legendary **Jazz Club La Zorra y El Cuervo**, a subterranean club accessed via a red English phone box at the entrance. Operating from 10pm until 1am, this small venue has an intimate, exclusive and Ronnie Scott's-esque feel and hosts renowned Cuban musicians.

6 Late-night Party Hub

While La Zorra y El Cuervo has been an iconic institution for decades, there is another basement club across the road, relatively new on the scene, that has also become a staple in Vedado's nightlife, although with a very different vibe. **Club 23** is where more affluent young Cubans like to party and listen to electronic music until 6am.

EXPERIENCES

Visit a Museum & Magnificent Mansion

MUSEUM

MAP: 1 P92 **H3**

Without a doubt one of the best museums in Havana and thus in Cuba, **Museo Napoleónico** contains a magnificently laid-out collection of 7000 objects associated with the life of Napoleon Bonaparte, amassed by Cuban sugar baron Julio Lobo and politician Orestes Ferrara. Although the collection is impressive, the highlight of the museum is the building itself, a gorgeous mansion with stunning stained-glass, library, sculptures and tiling.

Find out all about Fidel

MUSEUM

MAP: 2 P92 **D3**

Propagandist and proud of it, **Centro Fidel Castro Ruz** *(centrofidel.cu)* is a superb museum and cultural center encased in a gorgeous eclectic mansion on Av Paseo. It offers an encyclopedic insight into the life and times of the man who ignited the Cuban Revolution. Objectivity isn't really the aim here – instead, what you get is an uncritical homage to Fidel, beautifully laid out over two floors, a fecund garden and several affiliated buildings.

Pass through Parque Lennon

PARK

MAP: 3 P92 **C4**

If you prefer John Lennon to commie king Vladimir Lenin (both 20th-century personalities have a park named after them in Havana), decamp to this small square of green in Vedado, where a hyperrealistic statue of the former Beatle – unveiled by Fidel Castro on the 20th anniversary of Lennon's death – takes center stage.

UNDERSTANDING MARTÍ

A basic knowledge of José Martí and his far-reaching influence is crucial to understanding contemporary Cuba. Poet, journalist, philosopher, he was the brains behind Cuba's Second Independence War and remains the one figure who binds Cubans worldwide; a potent unifying force in a people fractiously divided by politics, economics and 145km of shark-infested ocean. Born in Havana in 1853, Martí spent well over half his life in sporadic exile, but his absence hardly mattered. Martí's importance was in his words and ideas. He was responsible for forming the modern Cuban identity and its dream of self-determination. There's barely a village across the country that doesn't have a statue or plaza named in his honor.

Step into Havana's Decorative Past

MUSEUM

MAP: 4 P92 E3

One of Havana's best museums dazzles like a European stately home. **Museo de Artes Decorativas** is replete with all manner of architectural features, including rococo furniture, Chinese screens and an art deco bathroom. Equally interesting is the building itself, which is of French design and was commissioned in 1924 by the wealthy Gómez family, who built the Manzana de Gómez shopping center in Centro Habana.

Stroll down a Presidential Avenue

BOULEVARD

MAP: 5 P92 E2

Statues of illustrious Latin American leaders line the Parisian-style **Calle G** (officially known as Av de los Presidentes), including Salvador Allende (Chile), Benito Juárez (Mexico) and Simón Bolívar. At the top of the avenue is the huge marble Monumento a José Miguel Gómez, depicting Cuba's second president. At the other end, the monument to his predecessor – Cuba's first president, Tomás Estrada Palma (long considered a US puppet) – has been toppled, with just his shoes remaining on the original plinth. Interesting, Calle G was also known for being a popular hang-out spot for Havana's edgy youth, where rappers, rockers, skaters and *trovadores* used to mingle.

Promenade along Paseo

BOULEVARD

MAP: 6 P92 D4

Av Paseo is another majestic boulevard in Vedado, which is wonderful to promenade down. Notable sites along the way include **Casa de la Amistad**, a stunning blush-pink and orange former mansion, now a state building, and the residence of the UK ambassador, which you may be able to steal a glance at through the fencing. This property is back-to-back with the North Korean Embassy.

Visit yet another Historic Hotel

HISTORIC HOTEL

MAP: 7 P92 H2

This classic modernist hotel – the former Havana Hilton – was commandeered by Fidel Castro's revolutionaries in 1959 just nine months after it had opened, and promptly renamed **Hotel Habana Libre** (*melia.com/en/hotels/cuba/havana/tryp-habana-libre*). During the first few months of the revolution, Castro ruled the country from a luxurious suite on the 24th floor.

Marvel at a Monument on the Malecón

MONUMENT

MAP: 8 P92 G1

West of Hotel Nacional (p94) is **Monumento a las Víctimas del Maine** (1926) to the 266 American marines who were killed when the battleship USS Maine blew up mysteriously in Havana harbor in 1898. The American eagle that once sat on top was decapitated soon after the 1959 revolution. Despite rumors to this effect, its replacement in the form of a dove sculpted by Pablo Picasso never materialized.

Enjoy an Unexpected Urban Oasis

BOTANICAL GARDEN

MAP: 9 P92 **H4**

Quinta de los Molinos is the former residence of Independence War general Máximo Gómez, a stately 'country house' that sits in a lush, wooded park that has been managed as botanical gardens since 1839. The main house, called the Casa del Verano, opened as a museum in 2022 focusing mainly on Gómez' deeds in the Independence War of 1895–98.

Sneak a Peek at Havana's Most Controversial Building

EMBASSY BUILDING

MAP: 10 P92 **F1**

Arguably the world's most famous **US embassy** *(cu.usembassy.gov)*, this modernist seven-story building on the Malecón, with its high security fencing, first opened in 1953, but it closed abruptly in 1961 when the US and Cuba cut diplomatic relations. It reopened as the US Interests Section, set up by the Carter administration in 1977, and in July 2015 it was rebranded an embassy thanks to the political thaw instigated by the Obama administration. The US withdrew almost all its workers in 2018, after several personnel began complaining of mysterious symptoms such as headaches, dizziness and strange sounds, fearing it was linked to sonic attacks or surveillance. The US Embassy reopened in 2022 and the symptoms have long subsided, but the world is still not clear on what caused what has been dubbed the Havana Syndrome.

Experience a Cuban Cinema Night

CINEMA

MAP: 11 P92 **G2**

Cine Yara is arguably Havana's finest movie house, host to many a Cuban date night, and a good place to get up to speed with the nation's dynamic film culture while fine-tuning your Spanish.

Scale Havana's (Second) Tallest Skyscraper

ICONIC BUILDING

MAP: 12 P92 **G1**

Unmissable on the Havana skyline, the modernist **Edificio Focsa** was built between 1954 and 1956 in a record 28 months using pioneering computer technology. In 1999, it was listed as one of the seven modern engineering wonders of Cuba. With 39 floors housing 373 apartments, on its completion it was the second-largest concrete structure of its type in the world, built entirely without the use of cranes. Once the tallest building in the city, it has now been overtaken by hotel Torre K-23 up the road.

Treat yourself to a Scoop of Ice Cream
ICE-CREAM PARLOR

MAP: 13 P92 **G2**

Despite the ebb and flow of tourism in recent years, ice-cream parlor **Coppelia**, slap-bang in the middle of commercial Vedado, remains a quintessentially local stronghold. The intricacies of the queueing system can be confusing to unversed visitors, but with some Cuban pesos and a few words of Spanish you'll be warmly welcomed into the fold. It won't be the best ice cream you've ever had, but the location is iconic.

Go for a Cycle
BIKE RENTAL

MAP: 14 P92 **B5**

Ruta Bikes *(rutabikes.com)* was Havana's first proper bicycle-hire and tour company when it started in 2013. Its cycling tours have proven to be consistently popular, particularly the three-hour classic city ride, which takes in Bosque de la Habana, Plaza Vieja, Plaza de la Revolución and the Malecón. Book via phone or email at least a day ahead. Kids welcome.

Go Grocery Shopping at a Local 'Agro'
FOOD MARKET

MAP: 15 P92 **E3**

Mercado Agropecuario 19 y B is Havana's most well-known fruit and veg market (locals complain it's the most expensive) and is a great place to wander through to see how Cubans get their groceries. Fresh produce is piled high and you're likely to strike up a conversation with a chatty seller. It's best to come in the morning and during midweek (it's closed on Monday and quiet on the weekends).

Educate yourself in Latin American Culture
CULTURAL VENUE

MAP: 16 P92 **D1**

Casa de las Américas is a prestigious institution dedicated to promoting Latin American and Caribbean culture through courses, exhibitions and events. Wander around its Galería Latinoamericana, browse the library archives, and you may come across poetry readings, talks or live music.

Visit Havana's Chinese Cemetery
CEMETERY

MAP: 17 P92 **C6**

Although almost all the Chinese population (over 150,000) left Cuba after 1960, there are an estimated 114,000 Cubans with Chinese heritage. Apart from Barrio Chino, another important reminder of this part of Cuba's history is the **Cementerio Chino**. Located close to Vedado's main Catholic cemetery and marked by a yellow gabled archway with Chinese lettering, this burial ground and national monument was founded in 1893 to offer a final resting place for the Asian immigrant population that settled in the city. As well as graves, statues, and vaults, some simple and some more grand, catacombs contain thousands of boxes

Coppelia (p109)
SANDRA FOYT/SHUTTERSTOCK

filled with remains of the deceased, a solution to the overcrowding in the cemetery at the time.

Glimpse into a Top Dance School

DANCE SCHOOL

MAP: 18 P92 C3

Acosta Danza is a contemporary dance company founded in 2015 by renowned Cuban ballet dancer and choreographer Carlos Acosta. Following his retirement from the Royal Ballet in 2016, Acosta established the company to help nurture the next generation of emerging dancing talent in the city. With large glass windows you can often see dancers stretching or doing barre work.

Workshop at a Community Cultural Project

CULTURAL VENUE

MAP: 19 P92 C5

El Cimarrón is a family-run farm-to-table restaurant and social project that hosts evening music and organizes cooking and dance classes. El Cimarrón (the name means 'runaway enslaved person') wears many hats and succeeds on every level. There's a strong Afro-Cuban vibe in the art, bamboo furniture and percussive instruments. Open or private classes include folkloric, rumba, capoeira and salsa, and in high season (November to March) they put on Afro-Cuban-themed dance performances with top dancers.

Best Places for...

$ Budget $$ Midrange $$$ Top End

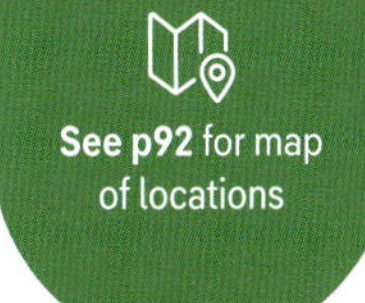
See p92 for map of locations

Eating

Cafes & Breakfasts

Kanda $$

20 G2
A coffee shop that feels more European than Cuban but is full of locals. Grab a pastry and a matcha coffee. *9am-9pm*

Cuba Libro $

21 B6
The most well-known cafe in Vedado, which doubles as a bilingual library. Select a book to read while sipping on an espresso. *10am-8pm, closed Mon*

La Bombilla Café $

22 C4
Choose from a selection of Spanish tortilla, pulled pork sandwiches, and crepes with honey and yogurt at this laid-back spot. *9am-2pm Tue-Sun*

Fangio Habana $$$
23 D4
This hotel restaurant does a luxury brunch menu with fresh smoothies, breads, pastries, granola, eggs and much more. *9am-3pm Sat & Sun*

Cafe Eclectico $$$

24 D3
Breakfasts with an Italian take on the pretty patio of chic boutique hotel Paseo 206 on Av Paseo. Think cured meats, cheeses, bruschetta and strong coffee. *7am-11pm*

Ela y Paleta $

25 E2
Mega-popular ice-cream parlor decorated with pastel colors and packed with Cubans. The dulce de leche flavor is out of this world. *10am-1am*

WAPA $$
26 D4
Another local favorite famous for its waffles, crepes, and its over-the-top, calorific ice-cream milkshakes piled high with whipped cream, sprinkles and chocolate sauce. *9am-11pm*

Casual Dining

La Mixóloga $$

27 G2
One of the best lunch spots in Vedado has utilized the tiny space by creating double-decker outdoor seating. They make their own bottled juices, and fantastic tacos and quesadillas. *10am-midnight*

GAIA $$
28 D1
Cafe dedicated to healthy options such as pastas, fruit bowls, quinoa and smoothies. It also does good club nights after dark. *10:30am-midnight, closed Mon*

Perro Swing $$$
29 B4
A gourmet fast-food joint with loaded French fries, Cuban sandwiches and mouth-watering pulled pork burgers. *noon-11pm Sun-Thu, to 11:30pm Fri & Sat*

El Tablazo $$
30 D2
A breakfast and lunch place on the seafront with great American-style brunches, French toast and baguettes. *10am-midnight*

La Chuchería $$

31 D2

A sports-bar vibe that feels more Miami than Havana. Cubans tuck into burgers and bumper sandwiches. *8:30am-11:45pm*

Camino al Sol $$

 C2

The completely meat-free Camino al Sol, while still a rarity in Havana, makes imaginative quiches, soups, pies and house-made pasta, and displays them in a deli counter out front. *9am-5pm Mon-Fri*

Luque $$

 F3

An understated Italian restaurant on Av de los Presidentes with vintage decor and decent pizzas and cocktails. *11am-11:30pm*

Panparapan $$

 C5

On the bustling Calle 23, this is the place to go to guzzle down pints of Cristal beer and enjoy a slice of pizza. *10am-11:30pm*

La Barraca $$

 H1

In the grounds of Hotel Nacional, this is a pretty good option as far as state-run restaurants go. Decently priced Cuban food in a pretty setting with the occasional peacock strutting past the window. Card payment only. *10am-11pm*

Fine Dining

La Bodega $$$

36 D4

A hidden oasis at boutique hotel La Reserva with a small but high-quality menu of gourmet dishes made from an open home-style kitchen. *noon-11pm*

Grados $$$

 F4

A small but pioneering restaurant where the menu is never the same and enthusiastic chef-owner Raulito Bazuk conjures minor miracles out of whatever's available at any given time. There's a strong connection to local farms and Cuban ingredients. *noon-10pm*

El Cocinero $$$

38 A5

Next to Fábrica de Arte Cubano, climb the old factory tower to get to this elegant and atmospheric rooftop restaurant with delicious small plates and sophisticated mains. *5pm-midnight*

Candela $$$

 F3

A Spanish-inspired tapas restaurant on Calle 23 y F with an ambitious menu. Top picks are the eggplant parmigiana and bombas catalanas. *noon-midnight*

Casa Mia Paladar $$$

40 D2

Clean-lined Casa Mia, abutting the Malecón, offers a simple Cuban menu, with highlights including melt-in-your-mouth pork cooked countryside style. *noon-midnight*

El Atelier $$

41 C3

With wall art, wooden ceilings and a terra-cotta roof terrace, El Atelier has an old school elegance and Cuban food with a French influence. *noon-midnight*

Totò e Peppino $$

42 G3

One of Havana's best Italian restaurants with two outlets in Vedado. Its pastas are a particular highlight, as is the service. *noon-11:30pm, closed Mon*

Tierra $$

 A5

Located within the complex of Fábrica de Arte Cubano, this rooftop restaurant offers a relaxing evening meal before you descend into the madness of the club-meets-art gallery below. Eating here will also get you access to FAC's VIP area. *8pm-1:30am Thu-Sun*

Drinking

El Bejuco

 44 B4

This has rapidly become a late-night favorite among Cuba's alternative scene. Swing in a hammock with a beer in hand and play a round or two of dominoes. *9am-4am*

Café Madrigal

 45 D4

A bohemian cafe and bar with ambient live music and good cocktails. *6pm-2am Fri & Sat*

Torreón de la Chorrera

 46 A4

A simple outdoor bar set around the dramatic ruins of a 17th-century tower floating on the Malecón. Expect to drink lots of cheap beer from plastic sharing dispensers. *noon-midnight*

Rylac

 47 F2

A small, late-night bar with a chilled-out vibe and edgy crowd, frequent live music, and good shots and cocktails. *6pm-3am*

La Vitrola Social Club

 48 E2

The sister bar of Habana Vieja's La Vitrola, the Vedado version has an equally vintage and musical theme with frequent performances from major Cuban musicians. *noon-1am Mon-Wed, to 5am Thu-Sun*

Pazillo Bar

 49 C3

A fun, LGBTIQ+-friendly bar with burgers, tapas, happy hours, drag shows, DJs and speed-dating nights.

Bar CapaBlanca

 50 H1

Jump in an elevator at Hotel Nacional and head to floor eight to a rooftop bar very few people are aware of. Expect stunning views of Vedado. *4pm-2am*

Shopping

AMA Havana

51 G2

Near Hotel Nacional, AMA is a daring Havana fashion brand owned by two dynamic female musicians. Their designs are bold, bright and barely there, made from multicolored beads and crochet. They offer workshops and talks, and have a small cafe attached. *9am-7pm*

Rama

 52 B4

One of several super-modern private businesses that seem surreal in time-warped Havana, Rama is a super sleek store dedicated to makeup, beauty and self-care. *9am-5pm*

Casa Belkis

 53 E5

One of Havana's best-kept secrets, Belkis' home is filled to the brim with antiques. Chaotic and cluttered, you have to really dig to find the treasures that are buried. You can find just about anything here. *hours vary, closed Mon*

Licorera del Hotel Habana Libre

54 G2

This liquor shop just to the right of the main entrance of Habana Libre is a great place to browse Cuba's many top rums. *10am-4pm*

See p124
for eating
and drinking
listings

Explore
Playa

Playa, west of Vedado across Río Almendares, is a large, complex municipality. Most of the sights are in Miramar, a leafy diplomatic quarter of broad avenues, geriatric banyan trees and fine private restaurants. Playa is most associated with elaborate mansions that testify to a wealthy past, although the city's most affluent still live here. The district's name means beach but its shoreline is rocky and rugged, worlds apart from the beautiful beaches of Habana del Este. Nevertheless, there are still fantastic restaurants and attractions along its coast. Further west lies Marina Hemingway, Havana's premier, if slightly decrepit, marina, and Jaimanitas, a fishing village that is home to street-art extravaganza Fusterlandia.

Getting Around

Taxi

Playa is a large and sprawling municipality that is best tackled by car. From Habana Vieja, a taxi to Playa should cost around US$10-15 depending on where you're going. If you want to keep costs down, you can order a moto-taxi (motorbike taxi) on La Nave app or try to get a public shared car from Parque Curita in Centro Habana or Calle 23/Línea in Vedado.

THE BEST

STREET ART Fusterlandia (p119)

INNER-CITY WOODS El Bosque de la Habana (p118)

SECRET SEAFOOD SPOT Santy Pescador (p124)

UNUSUAL ARCHITECTURE Instituto Superior de Arte (p122)

CUBAN CABARET Tropicana Nightclub (p126)

El Bosque de la Habana (p118)
ANTON_IVANOV/SHUTTERSTOCK

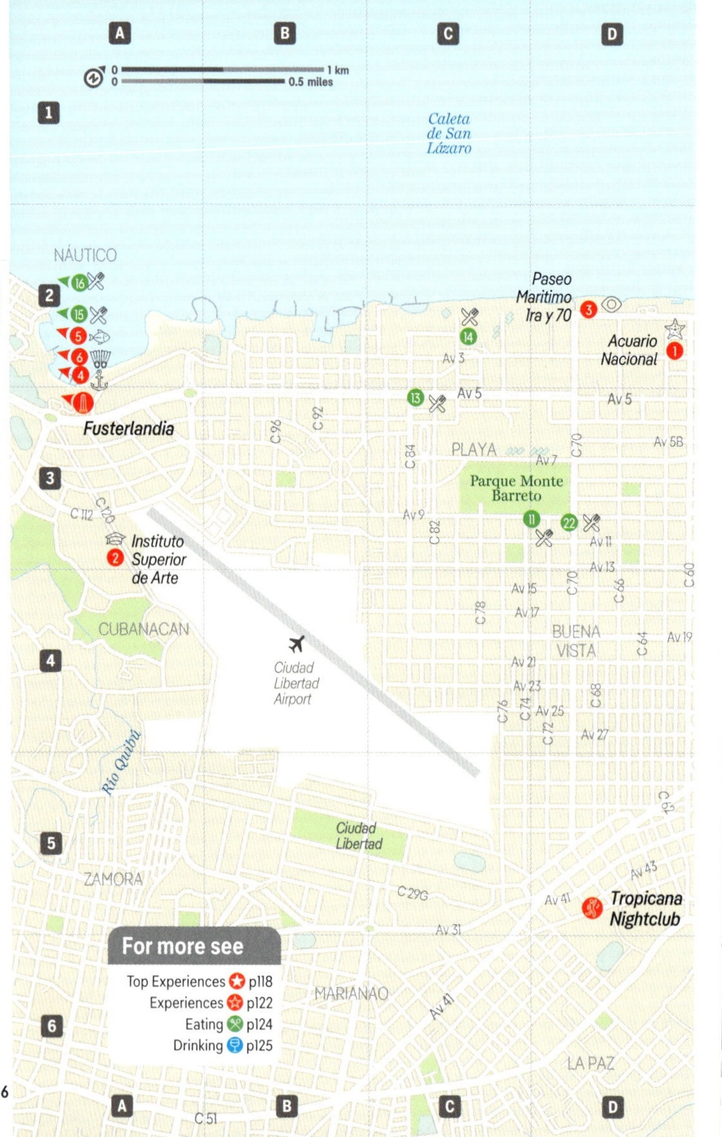
A
B
C
D
0 1 km
0 0.5 miles
1
Caleta de San Lázaro
NÁUTICO
2
16
15
5
6
4
1
Fusterlandia
Paseo Maritimo 1ra y 70
3
Acuario Nacional
1
14
Av 3
13
Av 5
Av 5
C 96
C 92
C 84
PLAYA
Av 7
C 70
Av 5B
3
Parque Monte Barreto
C 112
C 120
Av 9
C 82
11
22
Av 11
Instituto Superior de Arte
2
Av 13
Av 15
C 70
C 66
C 60
Av 17
C 78
CUBANACAN
BUENA VISTA
C 64
Av 19
4
Ciudad Libertad Airport
Av 21
Av 23
C 68
C 76
C 74
Av 25
C 72
Av 27
Río Quibú
C 62
5
Ciudad Libertad
ZAMORA
Av 43
C 29G
Av 41
Tropicana Nightclub
Av 31
For more see
Top Experiences p118
Experiences p122
Eating p124
Drinking p125
MARIANAO
Av 41
6
LA PAZ
A
B
C
D
C 51

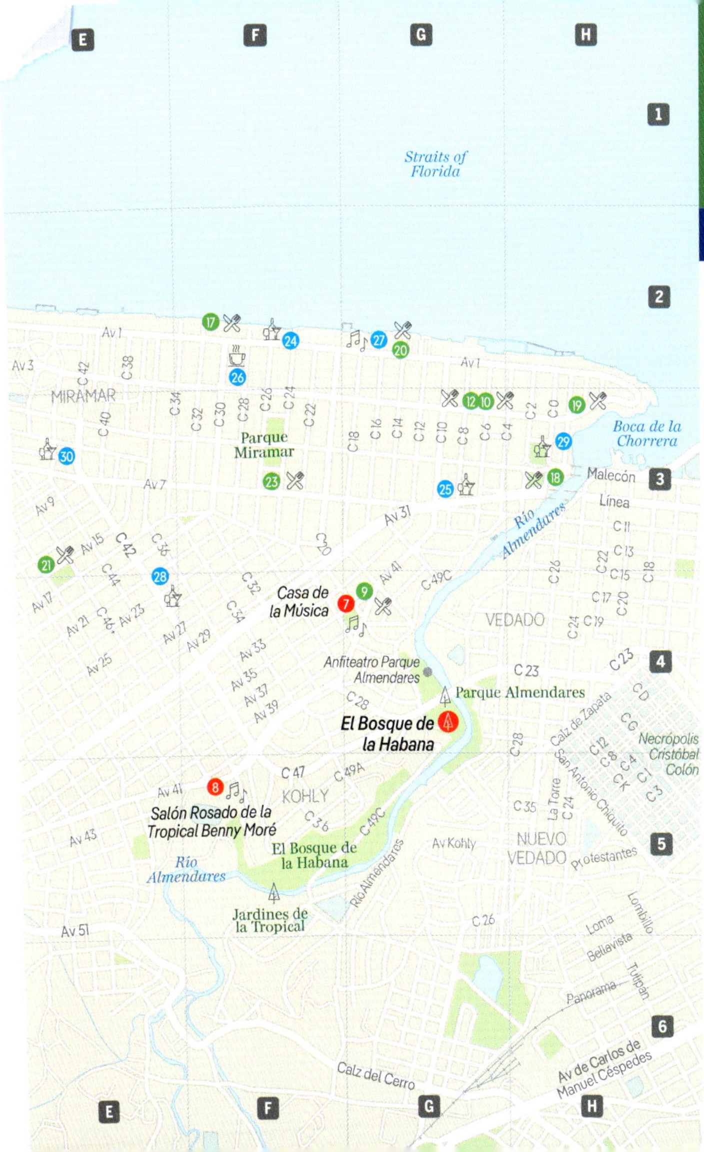

Straits of Florida

MIRAMAR

Parque Miramar

Boca de la Chorrera

Malecón

Línea

Río Almendares

Casa de la Música

VEDADO

Anfiteatro Parque Almendares

Parque Almendares

El Bosque de la Habana

Necrópolis Cristóbal Colón

Salón Rosado de la Tropical Benny Moré

KOHLY

El Bosque de la Habana

NUEVO VEDADO

Río Almendares

Jardines de la Tropical

Calz del Cerro

Av de Carlos de Manuel Céspedes

★ TOP EXPERIENCE

El Bosque de la Habana

Running along the banks of Río Almendares, on the cusp of Vedado and Miramar, the city's wildest woodland is a welcome oasis in the heart of the chaotic city. 'El Bosque' might not be as finely landscaped as the manicured parks of Europe, but it's a work in progress.

MAP P116 **G4**

PLANNING TIPS
The park is accessible from Vedado or Playa via taxi or on foot, crossing Puente Almendares on Calle 23. El Bosque is a sacred space, so don't touch or disturb offerings, and be tactful when taking photos.

Parque Metropolitano

El Bosque forms part of the wider Gran Parque Metropolitano de La Habana, which covers 700 hectares and is divided into various areas: **Jardín Botánico**, **Parque Almendares**, **Jardines de la Tropical** and **La Polar**, which can all be explored. The lower park (closer to the bridge on Calle 23) is usually called Parque Almendares and is more developed, with a stash of so-so facilities, including an antiquated miniature golf course, **Anfiteatro Parque Almendares** (a small outdoor performance space) and a kids' playground.

The Bewitching Bosque

South of the bridge is the wilder and more beguiling woods, with towering trees shrouded by hanging curtains of vines, giving it a secluded and eerie feel. Several paths wind their way through the greenery between the road and the river. El Bosque is an important site for Afro-Cuban religious rituals. Oshun, the deity of love and fertility in Santería, is often associated with fresh water, making the river cutting through the woods a special place for leaving offerings to the goddess. Expect to see devotees dressed in all white by the riverbanks, as well as animal remains, flowers, food and other unusual items strewn around the forest floor, a sign that rituals have taken place.

★ TOP EXPERIENCE

Fusterlandia

Head west to the seemingly low-key district of Jaimanitas, where artist José Fuster has turned his home neighborhood into a masterpiece of intricate tile work and kaleidoscopic colors that makes Barcelona's Park Güell look positively sedate. Imagine Gaudí with a Cuban accent relocated to a tropical setting.

MAP P116 **A3**

Neighborhood Entrance

Welcoming you to the Fusterlandia 'show' is the Jaimanitas neighborhood sign, with the words 'Homenaje a Gaudí' (Homage to Gaudí) arranged in a vivid mosaic. From here, Fuster's surrealist ceramics cover several city blocks, encompassing park benches, public spaces and more than 120 local houses. Bus stops, street signs and even a doctor's surgery have all been given an artistic makeover.

Taller-Estudio José Fuster

The centerpiece of the project is Fuster's own house. His home is decorated from roof to foundations with art, sculpture and – above all – mosaic tiles of every color and description. The overall impression defies written expression: the place is a fantastical mishmash of spiraling walkways, giant hands, cowboys with cartoonish faces and sunburst motifs arranged around a small pool. The work mixes elements of Pablo Picasso and Gaudí with stylized snippets of Paul Gauguin, Wifredo Lam, magic realism, maritime influences and aspects of the Santería religion.

The Bus Stops

Two local stops on either side of Quinta Avenida (Av 5) have been given the full Fuster treatment, with curvaceous profiles, toadstool-like roofs, and the stop name and number picked out in mosaic tiles.

PLANNING TIPS

You can buy art at numerous workshops around the neighborhood, including Fuster's own studio. For the best view of Fusterlandia, climb the observation tower inside Fuster's house.

WALKING TOUR

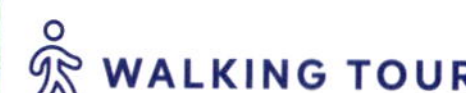

Havana's Fifth Avenue

Before the revolution, Miramar was a posh residential quarter where Cuba's richest people lived in huge, ostentatious mansions. Today, the dizzying cavalcade of fine eclectic architecture along arterial Quinta Avenida (Fifth Avenue) is home to embassies as well as other luxury attractions such as the old Biltmore Country Club and Havana's most splashy boutique hotel.

START	END	LENGTH
Casa de las Tejas Verdes	Club Habana	8.5km; two hours

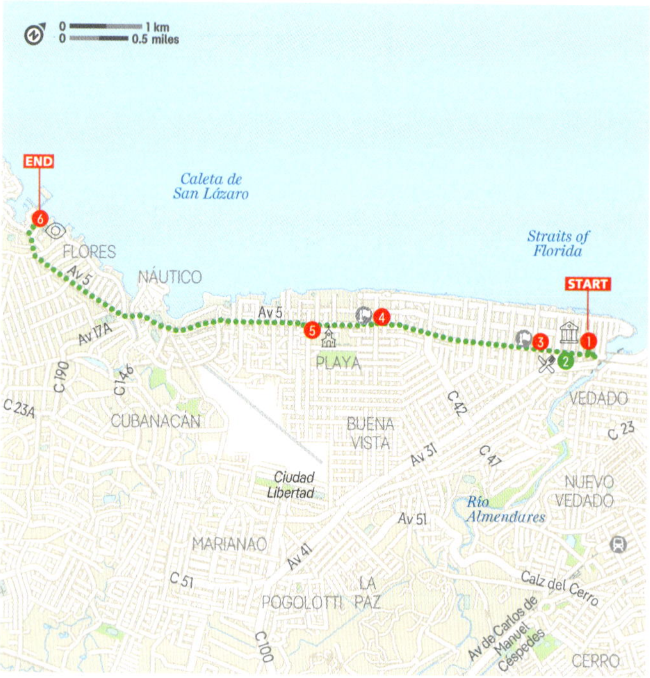

1 Green Giant

Emerging from the tunnel under Río Almendares, your first glimpse of Miramar is the Green Gables House. An eye-catching green tiled and turreted American-style *casona*, it is the only example of Queen Anne architecture in Cuba. **La Casa de las Tejas Verdes** was built in 1926, and for most of its existence was the home of a Havana socialite, Luisa Rodríguez Faxas, who lived here from 1943 to 1999. The house has been the subject of historical gossip, including that it was initially built for the green-eyed mistress Carlos Manuel de Céspedes. Today, it is a government building that offers tours by appointment.

2 Boutique Beauty

Havana's most flashy boutique hotel, **Casa Italia** perfectly balances Italian elegance with Cuban decadence. Its stunningly designed outdoor Italian restaurant, filled with plants and a grand pergola, offers a level of opulence that makes it a fitting place to go for lunch on embassy-surrounded Quinta Avenida.

3 Socialist Solidarity

Although there is not much to see from an architectural perspective, the importance of the **Venezuelan Embassy** lies in the historic alliance between Fidel Castro and former Venezuelan president Hugo Chávez. A large poster of the fellow socialist leader hangs at the entrance of the building.

4 Brutalist Behemoth

The **Russian Embassy** is impossible to miss. Previously the Soviet Embassy, this huge Stalinist obelisk that dominates the skyline halfway is a testament to the days when Fidel Castro liked to hobnob with Brezhnev et al. This grey giant is supposed to represent a dagger being stabbed into the ground.

5 Religious Icon

The hefty neo-Romanesque **Iglesia de Jesús de Miramar** is Cuba's second-largest church, built between 1948 and 1953. What it lacks in age, it makes up for in unusual quirks, including the nation's largest pipe organ and a head-swiveling series of 14 giant murals depicting the Stations of the Cross painted directly onto the inner walls by Spanish artist César Hombrados Oñativia.

6 Cuba's Only Members' Club

This fabulously eclectic 1928 mansion in Flores once housed the Havana Biltmore Yacht & Country Club. These days, **Club Habana** has swung full circle and it is again a popular hang-out for diplomats and affluent visitors. The club has a well-raked beach (technically the closest to central Havana), swimming pools (note plural), tennis courts, gym, bar and restaurant, all open to nonmembers for a fee.

EXPERIENCES

Make Some Fish Friends at the National Aquarium
AQUARIUM

MAP: 1 P116 **D2**

Founded in 1960, **Acuario Nacional** *(acuarionacional.cu/wifi)* is a Havana institution designed primarily for Cuban visitors, who arrive by the legion. Overseas visitors, be warned: the rather dilapidated facilities and limited selection of things to see are not on par with aquariums elsewhere. Sea turtles are the specialty, but there are also sea lions, crocs and dolphins, including hourly dolphin shows. Note that dolphin performances are widely criticized by animal-welfare groups, who say that captivity for such complex marine mammals is debilitating and stressful.

Check out a School Campus' Unusual Architecture
UNIVERSITY CAMPUS

MAP: 2 P116 **A3**

The leading art academy in Cuba, **Instituto Superior de Arte** *(isa.cult.cu)*, also known as El ISA, was established in the former Havana Country Club in 1961 and elevated to the status of institute in 1976. The cluster of buildings – some unfinished, some half restored, but all gloriously graceful with unusual arches, domes and red brick – was the brainchild of Che Guevara and a team of architects.

Enjoy Sunset in Ramshackle Beach Shacks
DINING SPOT

MAP: 3 P116 **D2**

This slightly raggedy waterside park sits in front of the large, ultra-modern Gran Muthu Hotel at the western end of Miramar's diplo district. **Paseo Marítimo 1ra y 70** consists of a cluster of privately run beach-shack-style restaurants that serve a variable inventory of seafood with sides of live music that can go on well into the *madrugada* (small hours). On weekends, these double-decker shacks are filled with locals, and its strip of coast and kids' play park make it perfect for families.

Dock your Boat in Havana's Marina Hemingway
MARINA

MAP: 4 P116 **A3**

Havana's premier marina, Marina Hemingway *(cubanautica.travel/en/destinos/la-habana)* was constructed in 1953 in the small coastal community of Santa Fé. After the Revolution, it was nationalized and named after Fidel Castro's favorite Yankee. The marina has four 800m-long channels, a dive center, a motley collection of shops and restaurants, and two hotels, and is only worth visiting if you're docking your boat or organizing water-sports activities.

Go Deep-sea Fishing WATER SPORTS

MAP: 5 P116 A2

Marlin Náutica *(marinasmarlin.com/home)* at Marina Hemingway runs four-hour deep-sea-fishing trips for four anglers for around US$330, including tackle and an open bar; marlin season is June to October. Catamaran tours of Havana's littoral are also available (four-person minimum).

Schedule in some Scuba Diving WATER SPORTS

MAP: 6 P116 A2

Between Marlin Náutica and the shopping center at Marina Hemingway, **La Aguja Marlin Diving Center** *(marinasmarlin.com/home)* offers scuba diving, resort dive courses and fullblown qualifications. Departures are at 9am and head out to water around Havana. A diving excursion to Playa Girón, where the diving's much better, can also be arranged.

PLAYA'S SUBNEIGHBORHOODS

The municipality of Playa encompasses half a dozen smaller districts. **Miramar** is the diplomatic quarter that begins across Río Almendares from Vedado. **Quinta Avenida** is Miramar's main drag, where eating and drinking places are close by. Miramar then fades into **Cubanacán**, Havana's one-time Beverly Hills, now known for its convention centers and yacht club. Things get posher still in **Flores**, home of the opulent Club Habana (p121) and Playa's only real beach. Western Playa ends in **Santa Fé**, which hosts **Marina Hemingway** (p122). Marianao is only visited for its world-famous Tropicana Nightclub (p126). Less heralded is the **Ciudad Libertad**, a former military barracks transformed into a massive school campus.

Experience Miramar's Iconic Music Venue MUSIC VENUE

MAP: 7 P116 F4

Launched with a concert by renowned jazz pianist Chucho Valdés in 1994, **Casa de la Música** is a Miramar favorite run by national Cuban recording company EGREM, and the programs are generally a lot more authentic than the cabaret entertainment you'll see at the hotels. It's a little suaver than its Centro Habana namesake.

Go Outdoor Dancing MUSIC VENUE

MAP: 8 P116 F5

If you're looking for something inherently Cuban, tag along with the *habaneros* to **Salón Rosado de la Tropical Benny Moré** for some very caliente action at this outdoor venue known colloquially as La Tropical. The long-standing club hosts live music and has changed its spots over the years – these days it's less Benny Moré and more jazz, with occasional reggaeton.

LISTINGS

Best Places for...

$ Budget $$ Midrange $$$ Top End

Eating

International Fine Dining

Otramanera $$
9 G4
A romantically lit garden bar and an inside restaurant with delicious Cuban-Spanish food. People often say its price-to-quality ratio is the best in Havana. *12:30-11pm Tue-Sat*

Toros y Tapas $$
10 G3
A top-notch Spanish-themed establishment with exceptional food and regular flamenco and music performances. The standout dish is the melt-in-your-mouth octopus tentacle (although it is pricey). *noon-midnight, closed Tue*

La Corte del Príncipe $$$
11 D3
A favorite among the most affluent expats and locals, its Italian food is hands-down the best in the city. Think focaccia, fresh pastas, and sharing meat and cheese boards. *noon-11pm*

Nero di Seppia $$
12 G2
Another very good Italian option, best for its Naples-worthy pizzas and delicately sliced carpaccio. *noon-11pm Thu-Sun*

La Catrina $$$
13 C3
Practically every menu in Havana has tacos now, but none are more authentic than at this Mexican restaurant. Enjoy corn tortillas and strong tequila-based cocktails amid Mexican decor. *noon-11pm*

Restaurante Italiano La Scala $$
14 C2
Located on the ground floor of the ambient Hotel Meliá Habana, this is a decent Italian restaurant with an air-conditioned indoor area and pretty patio where you can share a bottle of wine.

Seafood

Santy Pescador $$$
15 A2
Fidel's former favorite restaurant is tucked away along the edge of Río Jaimanitas in a two-story fisher's shack. Recommendations include the sashimi, tataki, seafood pasta and lobster dishes. *noon-midnight*

MAREA $$$
16 A2
A restaurant and beach bar serving Mediterranean-inspired dishes looking out over Marina Hemingway, where you can dive into the ocean directly from your table. In the shallow waters you'll find a romantic swing, trampoline and giant inflatable slide. *11am-11:55pm*

Arrecife $$$
17 F2
The best time to go to this upscale seafood restaurant is at sundown with outdoor seating on Playa's rugged shore. *noon-midnight Mon-Thu, to 2am Fri-Sun*

Amigos del Mar $

 H3

On the Vedado and Playa cusp, this secluded seafood restaurant on Río Almendares is an ideal lunchtime option. It has a big menu of every type of fish dish you could imagine. *noon-midnight*

Vistamar $$$

 H3

As its name suggests, Vistamar has epic ocean views where you can eat seafood and drink cocktails around a swimming pool. *noon-midnight*

Siete Dias $$

 G2

This seaside spot has a very decent menu, but it's really the ambience, location and view that make it so memorable. Housed in a beautiful mansion, the outdoor dining room-bar sits on Playa de 16, a lovely city beach known to anyone who grew up in Havana. *noon-midnight*

Other Playa Classics

La Cocina de Lilliam $$$

 E3

One of Cuba's first paladares set in a quaint garden area filled with plants and pretty decor. Excellent Cuban food with international touches. *noon-midnight*

Sensaciones $$$

 D3

This restaurant features exceptional ingredients, presentation and service. Its menu has a wide range of international dishes, from carbonara to crème brûlée and from black rice to burgers. *noon-11:30pm*

El Aljibe $

 F3

An iconic spot whose wholesome traditional Cuban food cooked on the grill, served with unlimited rice, beans, and root vegetables, is a rare find in Havana. *noon-11pm*

Drinking

Laid-back Bars

Café Fortuna

24 F2

A collector's cave of retro antiques, including floating car parts and other curiosities. Drink it all in while also drinking a cocktail. *10am-midnight*

Espacios

 G3

A late-night garden bar with tapas, pizzas, and frequent live music and events. *noon-3am*

Luly Bar Café

 F2

A coffee shop by day and a tapas bar by night, with light bites, beers, good wine and a friendly atmosphere. *8am-10pm*

Late Night

Don Cangrejo

27 G2

A state-run seafood restaurant hosting Friday-night concerts by the sea for a mostly young crowd. *10pm-3am*

Sangri-La

 E4

A basement bar and club with low ceilings that gets seriously packed and very sweaty. *11pm-4am Thu-Mon*

El Johnny Club

 H3

One of the most prestigious clubs in the city, El Johnny is a large indoor venue with an upstairs balcony to look down at the dance-floor action below. *10pm-6am*

Mio & Tuyo

 E3

A popular spot for young Cubans wanting to let loose. Expect dressed-up influencers and lots of reggaeton. *10pm-6am*

★ TOP EXPERIENCE

Tropicana Nightclub

An institution since its 1939 opening, the world-famous Tropicana was one of the few bastions of Havana's Las Vegas–style nightlife to survive the revolution. Immortalized in Graham Greene's 1958 *Our Man in Havana*, the open-air cabaret show here has changed little since its 1950s heyday, with flamboyantly clad dancers running through a potted history of Cuban music on a multilevel stage.

MAP P116 **D5**

PLANNING TIP
The cabaret opens 8:30pm and the show starts at 10pm. Tickets can go up to $120 per person, with a special New Year's Eve package costing $300

Scan this QR code for more information and to book tickets.

An Icon in the Making

Although it opened in 1939 in the lush gardens of the Villa Mina estate in the Marianao district, it reached new heights in 1950 when it was taken over by Martín Fox, a Cuban *guajiro* (countryman) who made his wealth from La Bolita (gambling). Part of this project involved commissioning architect Max Borges Jr to design the Arcos de Cristal (Glass Arches), a modernist structure comprising six concrete arches with panes of glass in between them that get smaller as they near the main stage, creating a spiral effect. Crucial to the design was the greenery in and around the club's structure, giving it an overgrown, tropical atmosphere.

Star-Studded Nights

During its heyday in the 1950s, anyone who was anyone went to Tropicana, both as performers and spectators. Nat King Cole, JFK, Marlon Brando, Frank Sinatra and Josephine Baker are just a few of the prominent names who attended its extravagant shows in the 1400-seater nightclub. Tropicana was known for its outlandish high-budget performances, choreographed by Roderico 'Rodney' Neyra, with accounts telling of exotic animals, ice-skating

THE CAROL M. HIGHSMITH ARCHIVE, LIBRARY OF CONGRESS, PRINTS AND PHOTOGRAPHS DIVISION VIA WIKIMEDIA COMMONS

rinks and dancers bathing in giant glasses filled with champagne. So popular was Tropicana that Cuba's national airline started offering 'Tropicana Flights,' promo packages that also included accommodation and admission to the club for American travelers. In 1956, they put on a 'cabaret in the sky' from Miami to Havana with dancers, drummers, trumpeters, a pianist and his piano all aboard the flight.

Tropicana Today

Tropicana was nationalized by the government following the Revolution, and since then it has kept its legacy as a top entertainment venue, although it's a lot less indulgent than in its golden era. Dozens of dancers perform in elaborate sequined and feathered attire, fusing Las Vegas with Afro-Cuban styles through fast-paced, dizzying routines and costume changes. Referencing Cuban musical legends, some of whom were regulars at the club, they tell the story of the island's musical history through dance.

FOOD & DRINK
There is the option to buy tickets that include a welcome drink, rum and dinner for you to feast before the show begins.

See p147
for eating
and drinking
listings

Explore
Greater Havana

Many visitors only venture as far out as Vedado or Playa, but beyond the city center there are a wealth of stimulating, off-the-beaten-track experiences to be had. Crossing Havana Bay are Regla and Guanabacoa, two marginal municipalities brimming with Afro-Cuban culture. Closer to the harbor mouth is Parque Histórico Militar Morro-Cabaña, containing two mighty forts that stand as a testament of Cuba's 400 years under Spanish rule. Further east, you'll find Playas del Este, a beautiful if slightly unkempt beach strip. Finally, heading towards the airport, are Havana's southern suburbs, home to Hemingway's former *finca*, the city's botanical gardens and some intriguing churches.

Getting Around

Taxi

To get to Havana's more far-flung areas, such as the southern suburbs, the only reliable option is by taxi. A taxi to Playas del Este costs between US$15 and US$20.

Tourist Bus

Habana Bus Tour's T3 bus runs every 40 minutes from Parque Central, passing by the Morro-Cabaña forts and terminating at Playa Santa María del Mar, from 9am to 4:20pm. The trip costs US$10 return.

Public Transport

You can get cheap *máquinas* (car shares) to Guanabacoa and Playas del Este that go from the side of Palacio de Aldama, just off Parque de la Fraternidad. Ask for either Guanabo or Guanabacoa and you'll be pointed in the right direction.

THE BEST

MIGHTY FORTS Parque Histórico Militar Morro-Cabaña (p132)

HISTORICAL HOME Museo Hemingway (p140)

CARIBBEAN BEACHES Playas del Este (p142)

AFRO-CUBAN CHURCH Iglesia de Nuestra Señora de Regla (p138)

VEGAN-FRIENDLY FARM Bacoretto (p145)

Playa Santa María del Mar (p143)

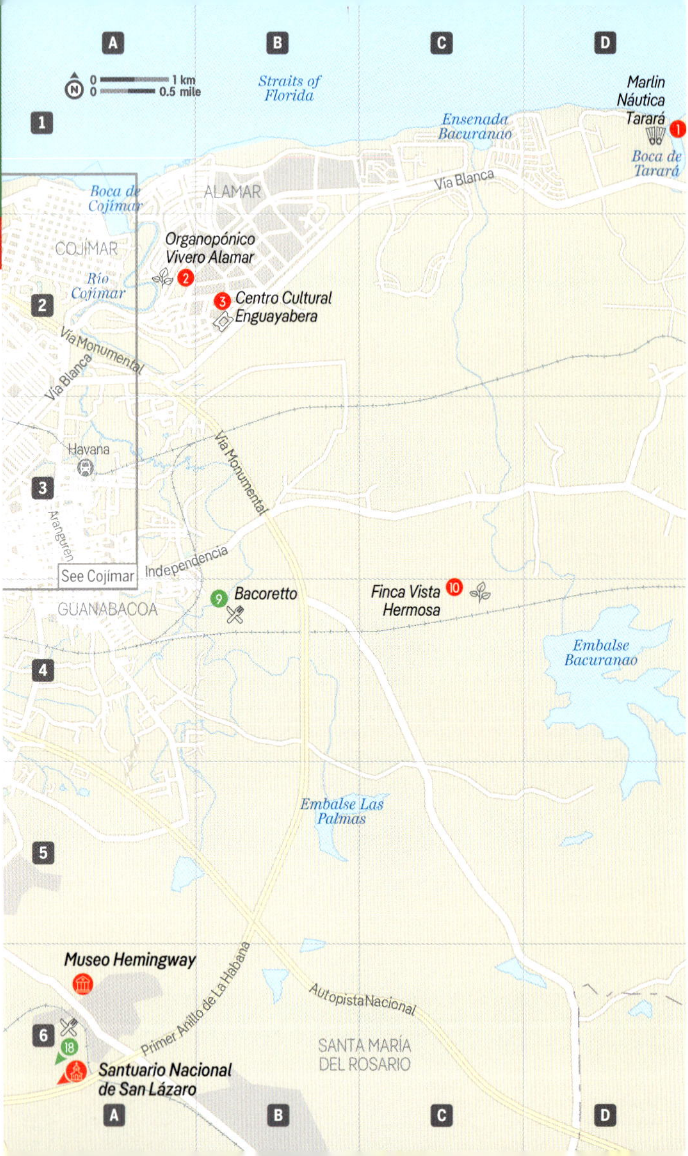

A
B
C
D
0 1 km
0 0.5 mile
Straits of Florida
Marlin Náutica Tarará
1
Ensenada Bacuranao
Boca de Tarará
Vía Blanca
ALAMAR
Boca de Cojímar
COJÍMAR
Organopónico Vivero Alamar
2
Río Cojímar
3 Centro Cultural Enguayabera
2
Vía Monumental
Vía Blanca
Havana
3
Vía Monumental
Aranguren
Independencia
See Cojímar
9 Bacoretto
Finca Vista Hermosa 10
GUANABACOA
4
Embalse Bacuranao
5
Embalse Las Palmas
Museo Hemingway
6
18
Primer Anillo de La Habana
Autopista Nacional
SANTA MARÍA DEL ROSARIO
Santuario Nacional de San Lázaro
A
B
C
D

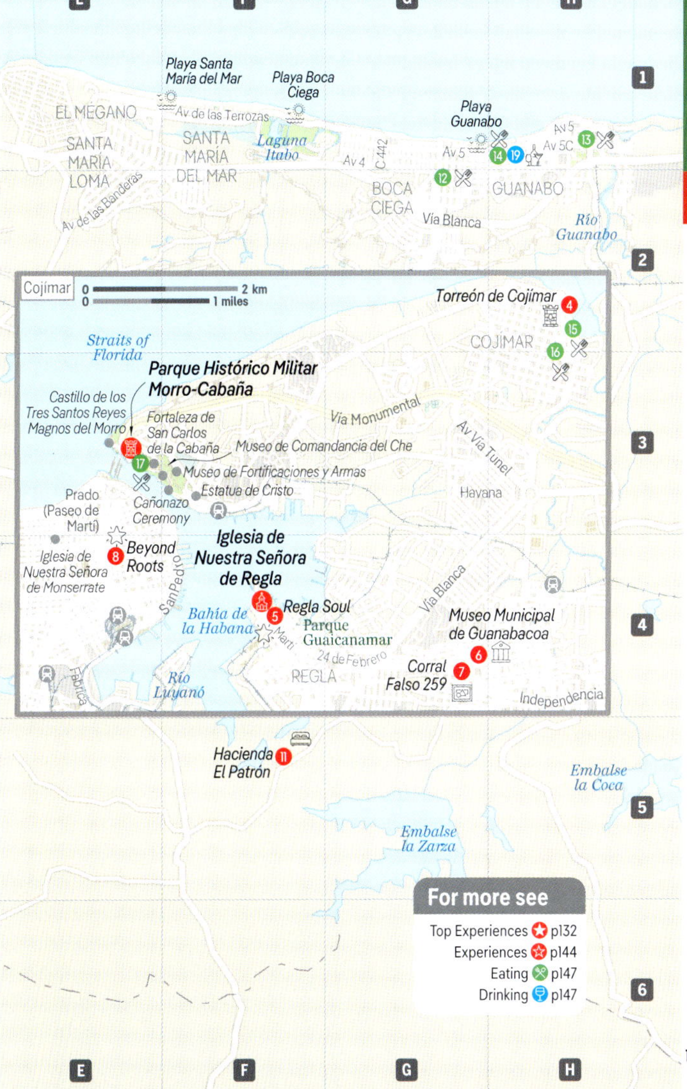
E
F
G
H
1
2
3
4
5
6
Playa Santa María del Mar
Playa Boca Ciega
EL MÉGANO
Av de las Terrozas
SANTA MARÍA LOMA
SANTA MARÍA DEL MAR
Laguna Itabo
Av de las Banderas
Av 4
C 442
Playa Guanabo
Av 5
Av 5C
BOCA CIEGA
GUANABO
Vía Blanca
Río Guanabo
Cojímar
0 2 km
0 1 miles
Torreón de Cojímar
Straits of Florida
COJÍMAR
Parque Histórico Militar Morro-Cabaña
Castillo de los Tres Santos Reyes Magnos del Morro
Fortaleza de San Carlos de la Cabaña
Vía Monumental
Museo de Comandancia del Che
Av Vía Tunel
Museo de Fortificaciones y Armas
Estatua de Cristo
Prado (Paseo de Martí)
Cañonazo Ceremony
Havana
Beyond Roots
Iglesia de Nuestra Señora de Monserrate
Iglesia de Nuestra Señora de Regla
San Pedro
Vía Blanca
Regla Soul
Bahía de la Habana
Parque Guaicanamar
Museo Municipal de Guanabacoa
Martí
24 de Febrero
Corral Falso 259
REGLA
Río Luyanó
Fabrica
Independencia
Hacienda El Patrón
Embalse la Coca
Embalse la Zarza
For more see
Top Experiences p132
Experiences p144
Eating p147
Drinking p147
EXPLORE
GREATER HAVANA

★ TOP EXPERIENCE

Parque Histórico Militar Morro-Cabaña

Making up arguably the most formidable defensive complex in Spain's colonial empire, this unmissable military park, part of the Habana Vieja UNESCO World Heritage site, comprises two strapping forts: El Morro, with its emblematic lighthouse; and La Cabaña, a sprawling military bastion famed for its sunset-over-the-Malecón views and theatrical cannon-firing ceremony.

MAP P130 **E3**

PLANNING TIP
Visit Morro-Cabaña during Havana's annual literary festival that is set in the grounds of the park every February, with families, book readings, talks, stalls and performances all taking place.

Castillo de los Tres Santos Reyes Magnos del Morro

Perched high on a rocky bluff above the Atlantic, El Morro (pictured) – the older and smaller of the two forts – was erected between 1589 and 1630 to protect the entrance to Havana harbor from pirates and foreign invaders (French corsair Jacques de Sores had sacked the city in 1555). The fort's irregular polygonal shape, 3m-thick walls and deep protective moat offer a classic example of Renaissance military architecture. For more than a century the fort withstood numerous attacks by French, Dutch and English privateers, but in 1762, after a 44-day siege, a 12,000-strong British force captured El Morro by attacking from the landward side. The Castillo's famous lighthouse, which you can climb up for a small fee, was added in 1844.

Fortaleza de San Carlos de la Cabaña

The impressively hulking La Cabaña was built between 1763 and 1774 on a long, exposed ridge on the east side of Havana harbor to fill a weakness in the city's defenses. In 1762, the British had taken Havana by gaining control of this strategically important ridge, and it was from here that they shelled the city mercilessly into submission. In order to prevent a repeat performance, Spanish King Carlos III ordered the construction of a massive fort that would repel future invaders. Measuring 700m from end to end and covering a whopping 10 hectares, this 18th-century colossus is the largest Spanish colonial fortress in the Americas.

The impregnability of the fort meant that no invader ever stormed it, though during the 19th century Cuban patriots faced firing squads here. Dictators Gerardo Machado and Fulgencio Batista used the fortress as a military prison, and immediately after the revolution, Che Guevara set up his headquarters inside the ramparts to preside over

Scan this QR code for the latest information about the park.

JOEL CARILLET/GETTY IMAGES

ARSGERA/SHUTTERSTOCK

TAKE A BREAK
Next to La Cabaña is La Divina Pastora (p147). With fantastic views and delicious Cuban food at great prices, it is one of the city's best state-run restaurants.

another catalog of grisly executions (this time of Batista's officers).

These days the fort has been restored for visitors, and you can spend at least half a day checking out its wealth of attractions, including museums, bars, restaurants, souvenir stalls and a cigar shop (containing the world's longest cigar).

Museo de Comandancia del Che

Museo de Comandancia del Che is probably the most interesting of the several museums spread around Havana's two eastern forts. It's a diminutive but nonetheless riveting exposé on the life and times of Ernesto Guevara de la Serna ('El Che'), and inhabits his old office in La Cabaña fort, from where he meted out revolutionary 'justice' in 1959. The story of his life is told with pictures and a few belongings (radios, rucksacks and guns).

Museo de Fortificaciones y Armas

Inside Fortaleza de San Carlos de la Cabaña, this armaments museum contains weapons from bows and arrows to giant catapults and cannons.

Cañonazo Ceremony

Every night at 9pm, actors dressed in full 18th-century military regalia reenact the firing of a cannon over the harbor in La Cabaña fort. In days of yore the shot marked the closing of the old city gates. It's a thrilling event with fire torches, showy marching and the deafening explosion of the cannon over the sturdy walls as the lights of Havana twinkle in the background. Wherever you are in Havana, you will hear the distant blast of a cannon, letting you know that the clock has struck nine.

Salas & Exhibits

Exhibits inside El Morro provide essential background on both forts within the military park, plus a perfect scale model of El Morro itself. There's also a room profiling the successful British attack on the fort in 1762, an episode that provoked the Spanish to build La Cabaña a decade later. The story is told through a series of painted canvases depicting the events of the battle, and is complemented by written commentaries in English and Spanish.

Nearby: Estatua de Cristo

This impossible-to-miss statue in the tiny Casablanca neighborhood, close to the military park, was created by in 1958 by Jilma Madera, who also designed the bust of José Martí at the peak of Cuba's highest mountain, El Pico Turquino, in eastern Cuba. El Cristo was promised to President Batista by his wife after the US-backed leader survived an attempt on his life in the Presidential Palace in March 1957, and was (ironically) unveiled on Christmas Day 1958, one week before the dictator fled the country. It was initially commissioned to be

GETTING THERE

You could get a taxi to the forts, but a more fun way to arrive is via Havana's public ferry across the bay. From Habana Vieja's dock, Emboque de Luz, you pay a few Cuban pesos and jump onto the boat, which takes you to Casablanca and its Christ statue close to the military park. This service isn't as regular as it once was, but if you have a little patience, it is a great way to travel like a local.

ARODEL/SHUTTERSTOCK

taller than Brazil's 35m Christ the Redeemer, but Jilma realized that a statue of those dimensions wouldn't have been possible in that location.

The statue, made from white Carrara marble, weighs 320 tons and stands at 20 meters. It faces the city with one hand in the air and the other on its chest, blessing Havana. The statue was hit by lightning three times (1961, 1962 and 1986) until a metal lightning rod was attached to prevent further strikes. As well as the sculpture, the views of Havana's cityscape from Casablanca at sunset and at nighttime are breathtaking and it's a favorite hang-out for the local youth.

TAKE A LOOK

On the statue, Christ's eyes are missing their pupils, so that it seems as if he is looking at you from all angles. He also has full lips, a reference to Cuba's mixed racial background.

★ TOP EXPERIENCE

Santuario Nacional de San Lázaro

Make a pilgrimage to Santuario de San Lázaro, a revered religious space that is of profound importance for both Catholic and Afro-Cuban religious traditions. Located in El Rincón, a small town about 25km south of Havana, this site is where they celebrate San Lázaro.

MAP P130 **A6**

The Sanctuary's Origins

Its history goes back to the 17th century, when it was developed a hospital for leprosy in Havana, where patients went to visit and pray. Urban development caused the hospital and church to move and be constructed in its current location in the early 20th century. Since then, the site has become one of the most important pilgrimages in the country.

Religious Syncretism

San Lázaro is syncretized in the Afro-Cuban religion as Babalú Ayé, the deity of healing and disease, stemming from both Lazarus, the leper beggar who appears in a parable of Luke's gospel, and Saint Lazarus the Bishop, who was resurrected by Jesus.

A Spiritual Spectacle

On December 17 (San Lázaro's feast day), thousands of devotees undertake a 5km pilgrimage to the sanctuary in Rincón from the town of Santiago de Las Vegas to honor San Lázaro and seek healing for themselves and their loved ones. Part of showing one's devotion is through self-flagellation. Many worshippers wear sackcloth and purple clothing (the color of Babalú Ayé, and of penance and sacrifice in Catholicism), and carry out the painful journey crawling on their knees, sliding on their backs, carrying boulders, shackled or dragging a cement block tied to their ankles behind them.

PLANNING TIP
Although the church is worth visiting all year round, December 17 is when you will get the deepest insight into Cuban spirituality. Look out for a fountain, whose water is said to have been blessed by San Lázaro himself.

Scan this QR code for more info on San Lazaro Sanctuary

★ TOP EXPERIENCE

Iglesia de Nuestra Señora de Regla

This modest church shelters the blessed virgin of Regla, worshipped by Catholics and adherents of Santería (who call her Yemayá) with equal fervor. The virgin's statue was brought to Havana in the 1690s and harks back to a devotional cult that originated in Spain in the 5th century.

MAP P130 **F4**

PLANNING TIP
For full Regla immersion, visit on September 7, the virgin's feast day, when the statue is taken from the church and paraded around the neighborhood.

Scan this QR code to explore the history of Regla.

The Church

The Regla neighborhood, with its strong working-class black communities, has been a cultural epicenter of Afro-Cuban religion since its inception. In Havana, there's probably no better place to see the layering of and transference between Catholic beliefs and African traditions than this church. The settlement of Regla grew up around a shrine first built here in 1687.

The church went through various incarnations until the current structure was erected in 1810, by which time the virgin had been declared the patron saint of the port of Havana. The chapel-like building with its blue wooden doors and heavy ceiling beams is colonial in style. Inside, alcoves reveal statues of the saints and a gold-leaf altar is dominated by a depiction of the black virgin in her customary blue robes.

The Venerated Virgin

The virgin, represented by a black Madonna, is venerated in the Catholic faith and associated in the Santería religion with Yemayá, the *orisha* (deity) of the ocean and the patron of sailors (always represented in blue). Legend claims that this image was carved by St Augustine 'The African' in the 5th

ROBERTO MACHADO NOA/GETTY IMAGES

century, and that in 453 CE a disciple brought the statue to Spain to safeguard it from barbarians.

The small vessel in which the image was traveling survived a storm in the Strait of Gibraltar, so the figure was recognized as the patron of sailors. In more recent times, Cuban rafters attempting to reach the US have also evoked the protection of the Black Virgin.

The Vendors

It is rare to find the church empty. Pilgrims regularly file in to pray quietly and offer gifts to the virgin. A semipermanent posse of vendors awaits outside the church selling flowers, trinkets and Santería dolls. Some of them lay out tarot cards and offer to tell fortunes. Many worshippers throw flowers, fruits and other offerings into the bay's waters to pay respects and seek guidance from Yemayá.

TAKE A BREAK
Across the road from Emboque de Luz, where you can get a passenger ferry to Regla, is Loft Bahia (p64), a tapas bar and restaurant with a sea breeze and view.

★ TOP EXPERIENCE

Museo Hemingway

Cuba wasn't just a passing dalliance for American writer Ernest Hemingway. The well-traveled novelist lived in the Finca Vigía in the tranquil Havana suburb of San Francisco de Paula for over two decades, starting in 1939. When he departed for the US in 1960 soon after the Castro revolution, his house was taken over by the Cuban government and later made into a museum.

MAP P130 **A6**

PLANNING TIP
The museum is open 10am-3pm Monday-Saturday, at a cost of CUP$12 per person. Don't come if it's raining, as most sights are outdoors and sometimes close in inclement weather.

The House

The main attraction at the site is the house itself, an attractive single-story abode full of natural light and open, spacious rooms. To prevent the pilfering of objects, visitors are not allowed inside, but there are enough open doors and windows to allow a candid glimpse of Papa's unusual universe. Not surprisingly, there are books everywhere (including beside the toilet), a large Victrola and record collection, and an alarming number of animal heads. The house's interiors are so well preserved it's as if he left just yesterday.

The Tower

The three-story tower next to the main house was where the author came to relax, ruminate and sometimes write. It contains a tiny typewriter, a telescope, a comfortable lounger and plenty of dusty books. The view north toward the distant city is suitably inspiring. Despite his passion for hunting, Ernest was a big animal lover and was said to have had 57 cats living in the tower.

The Pool, Pergola & Pilar

You'll need to use a little imagination to refill Hemingway's elegant swimming pool with water and summon up the ghost of actress Ava Gardner

DAMIRA/GETTY IMAGES

swimming in it. Two bathhouses on either side of the traditional pérgola contain interesting photos of Hemingway and his guests enjoying booze and book talk by the pool. One recurring character is Gregorio Fuentes, the first mate of Pilar and inspiration for the fisherman Santiago in *The Old Man and the Sea*. *El Pilar* was Hemingway's beloved wooden fishing boat that he once kept moored at the nearby village of Cojímar. Today it sits in dry dock next to the swimming pool on the site of the writer's former tennis court. Nearby is a baseball diamond and cock-fighting ring. With anti-American sentiment rising by the minute after Castro took power, Hemingway left Cuba forever on July 25, 1960. A few months later, the fledgling revolutionary government expropriated his property. On July 2, 1961, Ernest died by suicide at his new home in Idaho.

Scan this QR code for more info on the museum.

WALKING TOUR

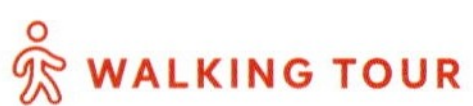

Havana's Eastern Beaches

Havana's Playas del Este stretch for 8km in an unbroken line from Tarará in the west to Guanabo in the east. While none of the strip carries the tourist-heavy all-inclusive atmosphere of Varadero, each parcel of sand has a distinct flavor, from LGBTIQ+ friendly Boca Ciega to the uncensored local scene of Guanabo.

START	END	LENGTH
Playa Tarará	Guanabo Village	8km; 3½ hours

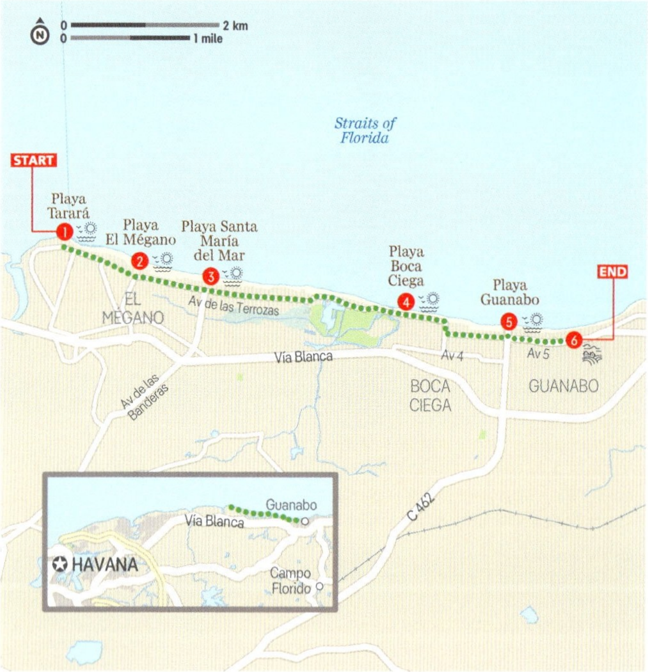

1 Gated Resort Town

The home of one of Havana's two marinas, **Playa Tarará** supports its own resort village, a sprawling cluster of 1960s holiday bungalows still used mostly by Cuban vacationers. Plush it isn't, although the adjacent beach is pretty and relatively quiet in low season. Known for its ocean whitecaps, the area is an under-the-radar kiteboarding nexus.

2 Beautiful Beach Stop

Playa El Mégano, where the fun starts, is popular enough to justify its own *punto náutico* (stand renting out beach toys), but sufficiently detached to avoid the screaming reggaeton sometimes heard further east. The local restaurant can arrange to bring your lunch out to you on the sand.

3 Tourist Favorite

Playas del Este's most popular beach and the most postcard-perfect. Three main beach hotels line **Playa Santa María del Mar**, a high-quality stretch of white sand protected by low dunes and shaded by occasional stands of palms. Various *punto náuticos* rent out beach kayaks, banana boats and other water toys, as well as beach umbrellas and sun loungers. Don't expect Miami- or even Varadero-style infrastructure. Shacks will fortify you with booze and seafood, and kiosks offer beer, canned sodas, and sometimes cheap fried chicken.

4 Gay-Friendly Beach

The dunes get higher as you approach **Playa Boca Ciega**, a broad beach abutting a small river mouth and lagoon. Since the 1990s, one part of the strip, Mi Cayito, has been known as Havana's unofficial (and Cuba's only) LGBTIQ+ beach, but those in the know also come for a more exclusive and secluded vibe and good service from the local beach shack. A rainbow flag proudly stands at the beach's entrance and in good weather the water is a luminous turquoise and invitingly swimmable.

5 Local Beach Spot

Backed by the small, scruffy beach town of Guanabo, the eastern stretch of **Playa Guanabo** is a little stonier and not as well maintained as the others. The bonus is the lively town that abuts it. While there's no fancy promenade, you'll encounter local life aplenty.

6 Beach Village

Low-rise **Guanabo** is a bona fide Cuban village, with shops, bars, restaurants and rentals, even though some are on the shabby side. This is a top holiday destination for locals wanting a beach experience without the expense of Varadero.

EXPERIENCES

Engage in Water-Based Activities
WATER SPORTS

MAP: 1 P130 D1

Yacht charters, deep-sea fishing and scuba diving are offered at **Marlin Náutica Tarará** *(cubanautica.travel/en/destinos/la-habana)*, 22km east of Havana, although services can be sporadic. It's generally best to check ahead at a hotel tour desk in Havana before heading out. Prices are similar to those at Marina Hemingway.

Amble through Alamar
NEIGHBORHOOD

MAP: 2 P130 A2

East across the river from Cojímar is a large housing estate of prefabricated apartment blocks constructed from 1971 by *micro-brigadas* (small armies of workers who built post-revolution housing). Alamar is the birthplace of Cuban rap and the home of one of Cuba's largest and most successful urban agricultural gardens, the **Organopónico Vivero Alamar**.

Experience a Local Cultural Hang-out Spot
CULTURAL VENUE

MAP: 3 P130 B2

Centro Cultural Enguayabera is housed in an old shirt factory abandoned in the 1990s, when it became a rubbish dump and public urinal. This state-sponsored community arts project in Alamar was inspired by Fábrica de Arte Cubano (p98) in Vedado. Numerous funky venues are bivouacked under its cultural umbrella, including three small cinemas, a literary cafe, a theater and a crafts outlet.

Follow in Hemingway's Footsteps
FISHING VILLAGE

MAP: 4 P130 H2

Cojímar is a tiny fishing village that's most famous for its Ernest Hemingway connections. In the 1940s and '50s, the American writer kept his prized fishing boat *El Pilar* moored here, and it's where he set his Nobel Prize–winning fishing tale, *The Old Man and the Sea*. The village also harbors a small waterside castle dating from 1649. Known as the **Torreón de Cojímar**, the fort was shelled by the British in 1762 on their way to capturing Havana from the Spanish.

Immerse yourself in an Agritourism Program
AGRITOURISM

MAP: 5 P130 F4

A few blocks from Regla's church, **Regla Soul** *(reglasoul.com)* is a cultural project created by local activist and Cuban hiphop legend Alexey and his partner Amberly, a US filmmaker with Afro-Caribbean roots. They offer immersive programs to tourists centered around sustainable agriculture, urban farming and food security, a critical topic in Cuban society today. Apart from spending time in Regla, enrolees visit various agribusinesses and eco-friendly initiatives in and around the city. They also provide workshops for the local Regla community to promote urban gardening and Afro-Cuban medicinal plants and herbal remedies, and have their own community garden.

Discover Santería from the Source

MUSEUM

MAP: 6 P130 **G4**

Opened in 1964, **Museo Municipal de Guanabacoa** was the first of its kind in Cuba, whose brilliantly curated collections and exhibits pay homage to the history and culture of Afro-Cuban faiths. Although the museum is currently closed to the public, local art curator and historian Marta *(Whatsapp +53 54326704)* can organize private visits to the museum as part of her Guanabacoan history and culture tour.

Pay a Visit to an Exceptional Art Space

ART GALLERY

MAP: 7 P130 **G4**

Welcome to **Corral Falso 259** *(instagram.com/corralfalso.259)*, the gallery, studio and home of the Cuban sculptor and painter Tomás Johnny Núñez. He collects discarded industrial and architectural objects, and creates large installations and sculptures that explore the themes of memory, the past and spirituality in Cuba. The gallery's surrounding gardens are also beautiful to sit in for a drink, with the occasional peacock roaming.

Absorb yourself in Afro-Cuban Culture

ETHICAL TOURISM

MAP: 8 P130 **E4**

Beyond Roots *(beyondroots.net)* is one of the most successful Cuban startups in the tourism space. The company offers educational experiences to Guanabacoa that specialize in Afro-Cuban culture and spirituality. Thematic tours include Afro-Cuban cooking classes, dance and music workshops, and experiences that allow tourists to delve into rituals and religions such as meeting a *babalawo* (witch doctor).

Tuck into a Vegan Feast

AGRITOURISM

MAP: 9 P130 **B4**

Bacoretto *(instagram.com/bacoretto)* is a family business on the outskirts of Guanabacoa that specializes in artisanal flours made from gluten-free ingredients such as yuca (cassava), coconut, rice and banana. Their magical farm, Finca Los Naturalistas, is an overgrown paradise of fruit trees, crops and aromatic plants, all of which they put to use in vegan feasts for visitors, featuring plates upon plates of creatively put together colorful dishes of plant-based food. They are also starting to incorporate spirituality in the finca, offering meditation, reiki and massage.

Escape the City to the Countryside FARM

MAP: 10 P130 C4

Situated within Guanabacoa, **Finca Vista Hermosa** offers a mix of agriculture and gastronomy a short 17km drive from the city. Recognized internationally as a 'slow farm,' it places sustainable farming practices at the center of the business. The 60-plus acres of land are home to cattle, poultry, horses and all kinds of crops, including vegetables, sugar cane and aromatic plants. The on-site restaurant serves farm-to-table meals, featuring homemade cheeses, meats and organic produce all reared and cultivated on the land.

Indulge in some Cuban Glamping GLAMPING

MAP: 11 P130 F5

Around 30 minutes further east of Finca Vista Hermosa is **Hacienda El Patrón**, situated on the border between the Havana and Mayabeque provinces. This private business offers glamping experiences on its 20 acres of land. This is where Havana's richer residents go for a romantic getaway and stay for a night or two in luxury white tepee huts. You can also just take a day trip to go for a rustic gourmet lunch, fish and kayak on the lake, and partake in other activities on the land.

Get Lost in Havana's Botanical Garden BOTANICAL GARDEN

Don't expect huge greenhouses packed with exotic plants or flowerbeds filled with hundreds of types of colorful blooms, but the 600-hectare **Jardín Botánico Nacional** (MAP P130: see 18) does have some nice bits to walk and run around. The highlight is without a doubt the ornamental Japanese garden anchored by an artificial lake layered with lily pads, pagodas and a fountain. Locals come here with families and friends to picnic, as Havana is known for its lack of green spaces.

THE LOW DOWN ON HIGH-END CUBAN RUMS

Although Havana Club is the most prevalent rum in the city, there are also others you must try while in Havana. Black Tears is a coffee and chocolate dry spiced rum inspired by the Cuban classic bolero 'Lágrimas Negras,' a favorite among the capital's young artistic crowd. Although almost any Cuban will tell you the country's best rum is Santiago de Cuba, made in its namesake city's former Bacardí factory. Its eight- and 11-year-olds are held in particularly high esteem. Even more exclusive is Eminente, a newer brand on the scene, part-owned by French Moët Hennessy Louis Vuitton, which does an exceptional seven-year 'reserva' rum.

See p130 for map of locations

Best Places for...

$ Budget $$ Midrange $$$ Top End

Eating

Guanabo

Restaurante 421 $$
12 G2
On a hill leading into Guanabo, this popular restaurant has super-affordable large portions of seafood dishes. The pork ribs are also a succulent choice. *10am-10pm*

Chicken Little $
13 H1
Specializing in all things poultry as well as other classic Cuban dishes such as *vaca frita*. *noon-11pm*

Trattoria Zia Cecilia $
 H1
A decent Italian-esque joint with a proper pizza oven. *noon-10pm*

Cojímar

Restaurante La Terraza $
 H2
Another shrine to the ghost of Hemingway, La Terraza hosts hordes of Papa fans who are bused in daily. The food and mojitos are average, but the terrace dining-room views are beautiful. *noon-11pm*

Ajiaco Café $$
16 H3
This farm-to-table restaurant in Cojímar offers an exceptional menu of rustic Cuban classics, such as ribs in a barbecue-and-honey sauce, or a unique shredded-beef-and-plantain pizza. Also offers cooking classes. *noon-11:30pm*

Other

La Divina Pastora $
17 E3
A hidden gem of a restaurant next to La Cabaña fort, which overlooks Havana Bay. Although it's state-run the food and the views are impeccable, as are the prices. *noon-10pm*

Restaurante el Bambú $
18 A6
Located in the heart of El Jardín Botánico, this outdoor dining area provides cheap Cuban food and crispy cold Cristal with a backdrop of the park's beautiful Japanese garden. *noon-4pm Wed-Sun*

Drinking

Bar Kopas
 H1
With its luminous interior and open terrace overlooking the street, Kopas sports a street-level barbecue restaurant but is equally popular for its drinks and nighttime action upstairs. This being Guanabo, you can expect to see plenty of foreign men of a certain age and their Cuban companions. *8am-3pm*

LA BO
DEL

Havana Toolkit

Bodeguita de Medio (p66)

WANGKUN JIA/SHUTTERSTOCK

Family Travel

Havana is a colorful and stimulating city that will capture a child's imagination. Despite shortages and infrastructure problems, locals tend to be good with children and are happy to help you get around any child-related obstacles.

Is Havana Safe for Children?

For a Latin American capital city, Havana is very safe. Due to community spirit and neighborhood watchdogs called Comités de la Defensa de la Revolución (CDR), it's common to see local kids play out in the street until late. The biggest things to watch out for are uneven streets, litter and unprotected roadworks.

EATING OUT

High chairs in restaurants are almost nonexistent, although most wait staff will be happy to improvise. The food scene has improved dramatically in Havana, and places can offer simple and plain dishes such as pasta, pizza and chicken for fussy eaters.

What to Bring

Havana suffers from perpetual shortages of most items, so it's very important to bring everything you may need for your child, as it will be very complicated to buy on the ground. This includes diapers, medicines, hygiene products and baby food. If you can, bring extras to leave behind to local families you may meet who really need the help.

Transport

Car seats aren't required and are barely available; in fact many vehicles don't even have seat belts. Luckily, the lack of traffic and vehicles on the road means that accidents are rare.

Keep Cool

Havana is hot and humid, so don't forget items that will keep your little ones cool.

Stay Local

If you want your kids to experience local life, rent a casa particular (homestay); they often have pets and children to interact with.

ANDRIENKO ANASTASIYA/SHUTTERSTOCK

Accommodations

Havana has thousands of accommodation options, including flash hotel chains, stunningly renovated townhouses turned boutique casas, and humble homestays.

Where to Stay if You Love...

Being Among Architecture and History

Habana Vieja (p39) If visitors are only in the city for a short time, they mostly choose to stay in the colonial heart of Havana. Here is where most of the most important museums, galleries, restaurants and bars are concentrated.

We Love to Stay in...

Vedado (p91) Tree-lined and mansion-filled Vedado is perfect if you want to feel close enough to downtown so that you can still get in among the action easier but far away enough for you to retreat to when you need to recharge and get some respite from the chaotic sights, sounds and smells of Habana Vieja and Centro.

Being in the Thick of It

Centro Habana (p71) You either love or hate Central Havana for its overstimulating street life and noisy neighbors. But if you're after an adventure, there's no better way to understand local life at the sharper end.

HOW MUCH FOR A NIGHT IN

a casa particular
US$25-50

a midrange boutique hotel
US$50-150

a five-star hotel
US$250+

Being Uptown and Upmarket

Playa (p115) There's a reason why most of Havana's foreign residents live here. Playa is by far the most tranquil and exclusive area and home to numerous fine-dining restaurants.

Being by the Beach

Playas del Este (p142) Havana is blessed to be a capital so close to gorgeous beaches. After immersing yourself in the city's intensity, unwind by the Caribbean coast for a day or two.

Food, Drink & Nightlife

Allergies & Intolerances

Cubans aren't as food allergy prone as people in many western countries, apart from when it comes to seafood. The Havana gastronomy scene is still flourishing and venues are still learning regarding health & safety protocols. Only some menus will list allergens on menus.

HOW TO SAY

I'm allergic to... ***Soy alérgico/a a...***

nuts ***frutos secos***

gluten ***gluten***

seafood ***mariscos***

dairy products ***lácteos***

?

HOW TO ASK...

Is this gluten-free?
¿Este es sin gluten?

Does this contain nuts?
¿Este plato contiene frutos secos?

Is there a vegan option?
¿Hay una opción vegana?

THE RISE OF THE PRIVATE RESTAURANTS

Private restaurants, originally called paladares, were first legalized in the mid-1990s. The name (literally, 'palate') refers to a fictional chain of restaurants depicted in the Brazilian soap opera *Vale Tudo,* which was popular in Cuba at the time. These were typically set up out of people's homes and have since evolved into top restaurants.

Menu Shortages

Havana struggles with ingredient shortages so it's a common occurrence that some items on the menu won't be available. Ask beforehand, as wait staff tend not to tell you what's not on offer until you go to order.

HOW TO... Pay the Bill

Currency: The bills at state-run establishments and big hotels generally are paid by card at the official exchange rate (CUP$120) and private venues in cash in either in local or foreign currency. If you want to pay in the latter, ask the restaurant's exchange rate before you sit down *(a cuánto está el dolar/euro aquí?),* as Havana has a thriving informal currency market, meaning that rates can fluctuate, although they are always considerably better than the official exchange.

Tipping: Many restaurants add a 10% service charge but you can tip more if you've had an exceptional experience (service can be very hit or miss in Havana).

PRICE RANGES

The following price ranges refer to the average cost of a main course.

$ US$7 or less
$$ US$8-12
$$$ more than US$13

OPENING HOURS

Cafes 8am-5pm or 6pm

Restaurants Generally open late morning and close at 11pm, sometimes until midnight

Bars Noon-midnight, or until 1am or 2am

Going Out

The Overview

Havana has a diverse nightlife scene, where you can hop around the city going to a ballet show in the early evening, listen to Cuban jazz over dinner, dance salsa, rave to afro-house DJs and get down and dirty to some reggaeton all in the same night.

Where and when to go

There are only a couple of spots in Habana Vieja that are open until very late; **Yarini** (p67) and **Ley Seca** (p67). Vedado is the district with the biggest concentration of nightlife options, particularly popular venues include **King Bar** (p105) for reggaeton and **Club 23** (p105) for electronic music.

PIXEL-SHOT/SHUTTERSTOCK

HOW MUCH FOR A

café con leche
CUP$350

beer
CUP$300-400

main in an upscale private restaurant
CUP$1500-3000

main in a state restaurant
CUP$1000-1500

mojito
CUP$400-500

sandwich
CUP$750-1200

LGBTIQ+ Travelers

In 2022, discrimination based on sexual orientation and gender became illegal in Cuba, a progressive law in Latin America for LGBTIQ+ rights.

Where to Go

Havana's LGBTIQ+ scene has come on in leaps and bounds in recent years, with many gay-friendly bars and clubs on offer practically any night of the week. **Pazillo Bar** (p113) is a well-known bar which hosts drag shows, speed dating and other LGBTIQ+-themed nights. **King Bar** (p105) is one of the city's most popular clubs which started out as a gay venue (look closely at the letter K on the logo) although nowadays it's a place for everyone. Where the Malecón meets La Rampa (Calle 23) has been a gay hangout spot for decades, especially when there was a lack of welcoming spaces for the community. In 2022, Havana opened its first LGBTIQ+-friendly hotel, the **Telégrafo Axel** *(axelhotels.com)* in Parque Central.

Must-visit LGBTIQ+ Neighbourhood

Mi Cayito (p143) is the city's unofficial gay beach. Expect to find locals and foreigners from all walks of life and of all sexual orientations interacting here. Compared to other beaches such as Santa María and Guanabo, Mi Cayito feels a lot more secluded and less-frequented. Look for the LGBTIQ+ flag blowing in the wind.

STRAWBERRY & CHOCOLATE

The 1994 Oscar-nominated movie *Fresa y Chocolate* was instrumental in opening dialogue about homosexuality in Cuba. In the film, gay artist Diego falls in love with a heterosexual communist militant who is secretly spying on him.

CENESEX

Take a look at the Facebook page of Cuban National Center for Sex Education (CENESEX), founded by activist Mariela Castro, daughter of former Cuban leader Raúl Castro.

Havana

Being the capital, Havana is the most progressive part of Cuba when it comes to attitudes surrounding the LGBTQI+ community, and locals are generally quite inclusive and accepting. However, homophobia, especially from those with strong religious beliefs, persists.

Health & Safe Travel

Havana is not a clean city, but it's a fairly safe one. The most you'll likely have to contend with are scams, hustlers and general unwanted attention.

TOILETS

Havana isn't overendowed with clean and accessible public toilets. Most tourists slip into upscale hotels if they're caught short. Even there, restrooms often lack toilet paper, soap, and door locks. Take around your own paper and hand sanitizer. You'll generally have to tip the toilet attendant.

Safety

In 2018, at a conference in Madrid, Cuba was voted the safest country in the world for tourists. However, Havana has become less safe in the past couple of years due to economic and social hardship, with more thefts and muggings being reported, as well as a rise in begging. That being said, Havana is still a relatively safe city. More than danger, the biggest threat is getting scammed. Cuba's two biggest hustles are currency exchange and selling cigars in the street.

Drugs

Cuba exercises a very strict no-drugs policy for all narcotics, even for tourists.

Pharmacies, Hospitals & Medicines

Severe shortages in Havana mean most pharmacies will be all but empty. It is highly advised to bring all the medications and toiletries you might need. If you have a health concern, the best international hospital to head to is Cira García in Miramar, Playa. You will need travel insurance.

HURRICANES

Hurricane season in Cuba runs from June to November. Fortunately, the country has an excellent record in dealing with tropical storms.

QUICK INFO

Insurance

Travel insurance is mandatory in Cuba; random checks are sometimes carried out at the airport.

Water

Tap water is not reliably safe to drink.

Flooding

Havana has downpours and its low-lying areas can flood quickly.

Responsible Travel

Follow these tips to leave a lighter footprint, support locals and have a positive impact on communities.

Go Private

The biggest tip for responsible travel in Havana is to engage with the private sector as much as possible. Choose family-run casas particulares over international and government-run hotels. Eat in private restaurants, buy souvenirs in boutique stores and use independent guides. Not only will you be putting money directly into the pockets of hardworking Cuban people but the quality and service is typically better in the private sector.

Bike around La Habana

Renting a bicycle is an independent and sustainable way to explore the city. Companies such as **Citykleta** *(citykleta.org)* and **Ruta Bikes** *(rutabikes.com*; p109) can help you arrange.

FROM LEFT: CAROLYNE PARENT/SHUTTERSTOCK, SOYASSER VIA WIKIMEDIA COMMONS

OUR PICK

Vegan

Enjoy a vegan feast lovingly prepared by **Bacoretto** *(instagram.com/bacoretto*; p145), a stunning family farm in Guanabacoa with a plant-based and gluten-free philosophy.

Ethical Tourism

There are a few tourism companies in the city that offer immersive programs and experiences to curious-about-Cuba travelers that aim to empower and uplift marginal communities. **Regla Soul** *(reglasoul.org*; p144), based in Regla, is all about sustainable agriculture, and urban farming. **Beyond Roots** *(beyondroots.org*; p145), based in Guanabacoa, does educational tours on Afro-Cuban culture and spirituality.

Resources

- **cedacuba.org** Cubans in Defence of Animals (CeDA)
- **portal.ohc.cu** City Historian's Office, Havana

RESPONSIBLE DINING

If you want to eat healthily and sustainably in Havana, go for a meal at **Baracoando** (p89) in Centro Habana, **Ajiaco** (p147) in Cojímar and **Finca Vista Hermosa** (p146) in Greater Havana.

Give a Gift

Havana (and Cuba in general) is suffering from severe economic issues, material shortages and an energy crisis. In short, life is tough at the moment for the average *habanero*. Many tourists bring gifts for locals that they meet or stay with or donate to an organization. If you have space in your suitcase, bring extra toiletries, over-the-counter medicines (you will have no issue getting these through customs), school supplies, toys, clothing or anything else you can think of. **Give2Cuba** *(Insta: @give2cuba)*, **Corazón con Cuba** *(corazonconcuba)* and **El Trencito** *(@el__trencito)* are reputable social projects to donate to.

PUBLIC TRANSPORT

Ride like a local and reduce your carbon footprint by getting a *máquina* (shared taxi) which goes to and from **Parque Curita** (p83) through Centro and Vedado, dropping off passengers at points of their choosing along the way.

Climate Change & Travel

It's impossible to ignore the impact we have when traveling; Lonely Planet urges all travelers to engage with their travel carbon footprint, which will mainly come from air travel. While there often isn't an alternative, travelers can look to minimize the number of flights they take, opt for newer aircraft and use cleaner ground transport, such as trains. One proposed solution – purchasing carbon offsets – unfortunately does not cancel out the impact of individual flights. While most destinations will depend on air travel for the foreseeable future, for now, pursuing ground-based travel where possible is the best course of action.

The **UN Carbon Offset Calculator** shows how flying impacts a household's emissions

The **ICAO's carbon emissions calculator** allows visitors to analyze the CO_2 generated by point-to-point journeys

Accessible Travel

Accommodation

Many casas particulares, rentals and boutique hotels are in old buildings with many flights of steps, rooftops, and elevators that are regularly out of order. It might be better to invest in a higher-quality hotel offering accessible rooms with wide doors and customized bathrooms that can cater for travelers with disabilities.

Transport

With battered vehicles, potholed roads, and crumbling buildings, independent travel can be difficult for people with physical disabilities. Public buses lack modifications for travelers with limited mobility. For comfort and reliability, modern Cubataxis are the best way of getting around.

When it comes to solo female travellers, Havana is a relatively safe city, although walking around Habana Vieja and Centro alone at night is not advised. Perhaps the most inconvenient thing women may have to deal with are the incessant *piropos* (catcalls) of Cuban men in the street. Likewise, taxi drivers are chatty but can also get quite flirty. To combat this, **Brumpa** *(brumpa.net/brumpaApp)* is a female-owned taxi app, designed with women's comfort and safety in mind, with mainly female drivers.

PEDESTRIANIZED ZONES

Havana has multiple pedestrianized streets and walkways where you can move around in a safe, traffic-free environment. Calle Obispo, El Prado (Paseo de Martí), Bulevar San Rafael and Av Paseo are some examples.

Community Spirit

Cuba's inclusive culture extends to travelers with disabilities, and while facilities may be lacking, the generous nature of Cubans and their talent for 'working things out' generally compensates when it can.

WATCH OUT WHEN WALKING

Uneven pavements, steps and curbs are all a perennial problem in Havana. Habana Vieja has some cobblestone streets that make walking a little tricky.

Resources

• **aclifim@aclifim.cu** Asociación Cubana de Limitados Físco-Motores is an internationally recognized non-profit with a portal for when in Cuba. • **disabledholidays.com** Useful information hub for accessible travel that lists a handful of Cuban hotels.

Nuts & Bolts

Opening Hours

Banks 9am–3pm Monday to Friday

Cadeca money exchanges 9am–7pm Monday to Saturday, 9am–noon Sunday. Many top-end city hotels offer money exchange late into the evening.

Pharmacies 8am–8pm

Post offices 8am–5pm Monday to Saturday, sometimes longer

Restaurants Noon–midnight

Shops 9am–5pm Monday to Saturday, 9am–noon Sunday

QUICK INFO

Time Zone Eastern Standard Time (GMT/UTC minus five hours)

Country Code +53

Emergency Number 106

Population 11.2 million

ELECTRICITY

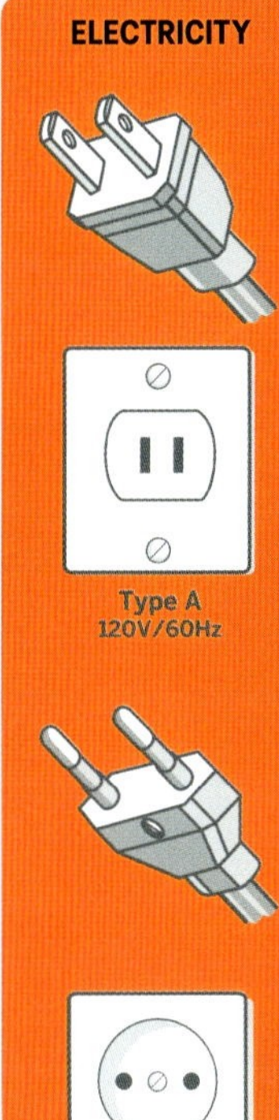

Type A
120V/60Hz

Type C
220V/50Hz

Internet

The Internet is still a relatively new phenomenon in Havana and it has improved considerably over the past few years. Most major hotels and upscale accommodation will have decent wi-fi but many places do not. 3G/4G can still be very patchy in parts of the city.

Public Holidays

Officially, Cuba has 10 public holidays where shops, banks and public and private offices are closed. Some private businesses may decide to stay open depending on the holiday.

January 1 Día de la Revolución (Liberation Day)

January 2 Día de la Victoria (Victory of the Armed Forces)

March/April (date varies) Good Friday

May 1 Día de los Trabajadores (International Workers Day)

July 25–27 Día de la Rebeldía Nacional (Commemoration of Moncada Attack)

October 10 Día de la Independencia (Independence Day)

December 25 Navidad (Christmas Day)

December 31 New Year's Eve

Abierto Open

Cerrado Closed

Language

Basics

Hello.
Hola. *o·la*

Goodbye.
Adiós. *a·dyos*

Sorry.
Lo siento. *lo syen·to*

Yes./No.
Sí./No. *see/no*

Please.
Por favor. *por fa·vor*

How are you?
¿Qué tal? *ke tal*

Fine, thanks.
Bien, gracias. *byen gra·syas*

Excuse me/sorry.
Perdón. *per·don*

Thank you.
Gracias. *gra·syas*

You're welcome.
De nada. *de na·da*

My name is ...
Me llamo... *me ya·mo...*

Fast Phrases

Do you speak English?
¿Habla inglés? (pol) *a·bla een·gles*

I don't understand.
Yo no entiendo. *yo no en·tyen·do*

I'd like... **Quisiera...** *kee·syer·a*
a beer. **una cerveza.** *oo·na ser·veh·sa*
a coffee. **un café.** *oon ka·feh*

Where are the toilets?
¿Dónde están los servicios? *don·de es·tan los ser·vee·syos*

Please speak more slowly.
Por favor, hable más despacio. *por fa·vor, a·ble mas des·pa·syoh*

What time is it?
¿Qué hora es? *ke o·ra es*

Can you help me?
¿Puede ayudarme? *pweh·de ah·yu·dar·me*

I'm lost.
Estoy perdido/Estoy perdida *(male/female) es·toy per·dee·do/per·dee·da*

I don't speak Spanish.
No hablo español. *no a·blo es·pan·yol*

Where is the bus station?
¿Dónde está la estación de autobuses? *don·de es·ta la es·ta·syon de ow·to·boo·ses*

Numbers

uno *oo·no*

dos *dos*

tres *tres*

cuatro *kwa·tro*

cinco *seen·ko*

Good to Know

The most common phrase you'll hear all over Havana is **¿Qué bola asere?** (What's up man?) Cubans are naturally affectionate, so other terms of endearment you'll hear are **mi vida** (my life), **mi cielo** (my heaven), **mijo/a**, **pipo**, **tata**, **titi**, **mami**, **papi**, and so on. Foreigners are called **yumas** (sometimes negatively, like gringo/a). And, where there's a **yuma** there'll be a **jinetero** close by, aka a scammer/hustler. Ask **¿El último?**(who's last?) When you want to join a queue and once you have, reply **'yo'** (me!) when asked the same question.

MORE CUBAN SLANG

Guagua Bus
Gao Home
Pincha Work
Permiso Excuse me
¡Sirvió! Sounds good!
Jamar Eat
Jevo/jeva boyfriend/girlfriend
Jaba plastic bag

Signs

Salida Exit
Entrada Entrance
Abierto Open
Cerrado Closed
Mujeres/damas Women
Hombres/caballeros Men
Baños (WC) Toilets
Aeropuerto Airport
Calle Street
Jalar Pull
Empujar Push
No fumar No Smoking

Listen For...

Su pasaporte, por favor. *soo pa·sa·por·te por fa·vor*
Your passport, please.

Su visado, por favor. *soo vee·sa·do por fa·vor*
Your visa, please.

THE CUBAN ACCENT

The informal, Caribbean feel of Cuban Spanish makes it a tricky accent to understand (just imagine an English language learner trying to comprehend a Jamaican). Cubans swallow many of their consonants: for example, the **d** in *cansado* (tired) disappears, becoming *cansao'*. The letter **s** at the end of a word is practically non-existent, where *gracias* turns to *gracia*. Similarly, the letter **r** can turn to **l**, so *amor* becomes *amol*.

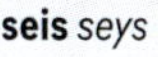

seis *seys*

siete *sye·te*

ocho *o·cho*

nueve *nwe·ve*

diez *dyes*

Index

Sights p000 Map pages **p000**

See also separate subindexes for:
Eating p164
Drinking p165
Shopping p165

Eating

Drinking

Shopping

Send Us Your Feedback

We love to hear from travellers – your comments help make our books better. We read every word, and we guarantee that your feedback goes straight to the authors. Visit lonelyplanet.com/contact to submit your updates and suggestions.

Note: We may edit, reproduce and incorporate your comments in Lonely Planet products such as guidebooks, websites and digital products, so let us know if you are happy to have your name acknowledged. For a copy of our privacy policy visit lonelyplanet.com/legal.

Acknowledgements

Cover photograph: Flower seller, Havana, XH_S/ Unsplash

Back photograph: Havana sunset, Diego Cervo/ Shutterstock

THIS BOOK

The 3rd edition of Lonely Planet's Pocket Havana guidebook was researched and written by Katya Bleszynska. The previous edition was written by Brendan Sainsbury. This guidebook was produced by the following:

Destination Editor
Alicia Johnson

Cartographer
Valentina Kremenchutskaya

Production Editor
Kate James

Image Editor
Fergal Condon

Assisting Editors
Peterjon Cresswell, Kat Rowan, Vicky Smith, Clifton Wilkinson

Cover Researcher
Katelyn Perry

Paper in this book is certified against the Forest Stewardship Council™ standards. FSC™ promotes environmentally responsible, socially beneficial and economically viable management of the world's forests.

Published by Lonely Planet Global Limited

CRN 554153

3rd edition – Dec 2025

ISBN 978 1 78868 859 8

10 9 8 7 6 5 4 3 2 1

Printed in China